Spelling Wisdom
Book One
(American Version)

Learn today's 6,000 most frequently used words,
presented in the writings of great men and women of history

Compiled and Edited
by
Sonya Shafer

Spelling Wisdom, Book One (American Version)
© 2006, Sonya Shafer

Published and printed by
Simply Charlotte Mason, LLC
P.O. Box 892
Grayson, Georgia 30017-0892

ISBN 978-1-61634-026-1

www.SimplyCharlotteMason.com

Contents
Spelling Wisdom, Book One

Contents (cont.)
Spelling Wisdom, Book One

Contents (cont.)
Spelling Wisdom, Book One

Contents (cont.)
Spelling Wisdom, Book One

Contents (cont.)
Spelling Wisdom, Book One

Contents (cont.)
Spelling Wisdom, Book One

Contents (cont.)
Spelling Wisdom, Book One

Contents (cont.)
Spelling Wisdom, Book One

Contents (cont.)
Spelling Wisdom, Book One

Contents (cont.)
Spelling Wisdom, Book One

Introduction

A Word about Dictation

Just as Charlotte Mason taught handwriting in the context of an interesting passage or text, so she taught spelling, not in isolated lists of words but in the context of useful and beautiful language.

We can present the child with a list of words to learn, such as: "am, will, can, I, ought." How much more pleasant to rearrange that list of words into an inspiring or interesting thought, like Charlotte Mason's motto for students: "I am, I can, I ought, I will."

Charlotte used this principle with prepared dictation to teach spelling, beginning in about the third or fourth grade. In prepared dictation, the student is given a passage to study before he is required to write it—the chief objective being to write it correctly.

Miss Mason believed that "the gift of spelling depends upon the power the eye possesses to 'take' (in a photographic sense) a detailed picture of a word; and this is a power and habit which must be cultivated in children from the first. When they have read 'cat,' they must be encouraged to see the word with their eyes shut, and the same habit will enable them to image 'Thermopylae.'"

She discouraged teachers from allowing their students to see a word incorrectly spelled, for "once the eye sees a misspelt word, that image remains; and if there is also the image of the word rightly spelt, we are perplexed as to which is which."

Of course, students will not spell every word correctly every time, therefore, it becomes "the teacher's business to prevent false spelling, and, if an error has been made, to hide it away, as it were, so that the impression may not become fixed."

"Dictation lessons, conducted in some such way as the following, usually result in good spelling."

(Quotations from *Home Education*, pp. 240, 241)

How to Use
Spelling Wisdom

1. Once or twice a week **give** your student a dictation exercise you want him to learn. Simply print or copy the exercise from this book. (You have permission to duplicate the exercises for use within your immediate household.)

2. Look through the exercise together and **identify** the words that you or the student thinks needs his attention in order to spell them confidently.

3. Instruct the student to **study** the identified words—one at a time—until he is sure he can spell every word in the exercise. This study period may take anywhere from a few minutes to several days, depending on the length of the exercise and the needs of the student. Set aside a little time each day for brief but consistent study of the exercise as needed. (See below for how to study a word.)

4. When the student is confident that he can spell every word in the exercise, **dictate** the passage to him one phrase at a time, saying the phrase only once. Pause after each phrase is spoken to allow him time to write it. Keep a careful eye on his efforts. If a word is misspelled, quickly cover it with a small self-stick note so its false spelling won't be engraved in the student's mind.

5. After the dictation is complete, the student should study any words that he misspelled and, when he is ready, **write** the words correctly on the self-stick notes.

How to Study a Word

You may want to work with younger or uncertain students to teach them how to study an unfamiliar word, as outlined below. Older students or students more accustomed to using the method below may study independently.

- Copy the word carefully, making sure it is spelled correctly.
- Look at the word until you can close your eyes and see it spelled correctly in your mind.
- Practice writing the word only if the teacher is nearby to immediately erase any misspellings.

Along with Charlotte's method of visualizing the word, we might add one or two study techniques for students who like to use their other senses in the learning process.
- Say the letters aloud in order while looking at the word.
- "Write" the word with your first finger on a sheet of paper or other smooth surface, being careful to look at the word and spell it correctly.

About *Spelling Wisdom*

When I read about Charlotte Mason's method of using prepared dictation to teach spelling, I loved the idea and wanted to use it. But I was concerned about missing some necessary words as I selected dictation passages to use. I felt very secure using my traditional spelling lists that I knew included the most frequently used words in the English language, which my children definitely needed to learn to spell.

So I decided to try to combine the two: dictation exercises that I could be sure included the most frequently used words in the English language. The *Spelling Wisdom* series is the result of that effort.

The five books' exercises become progressively longer and contain more difficult words as you work through the series. Each book contains 140 exercises. If you cover two exercises per week, you should be able to finish a *Spelling Wisdom* book in a little less than two school years. Charlotte began dictation exercises with students around the third or fourth grade. With that schedule in mind, here is a rough model of which books correspond to which grades:

Grades 3–5	Book One
Grades 5–7	Book Two
Grades 7–9	Book Three
Grades 9–11	Book Four
Grades 11, 12	Book Five

Content

The exercises cover a broad range of subjects and topics to reinforce Charlotte's love of a full and generous education. Because the books are not thematic, you can use and benefit from the exercises no matter what you may be studying in other school subjects.

I wanted to keep Miss Mason's high standards for beautiful thoughts and engaging narratives, so the sources of these exercises are speeches, letters, and quotations of famous people; excerpts from historical documents; descriptions of historical people and events; poetry; Scripture; excerpts from great literature; and selections from old readers and books for young people. Most of the passages were written prior to 1900. (I did find it necessary to write a few original exercises that involved the more modern words, like "infrastructure" and "computer.") Each book's bibliography and table of contents will provide more specific information as to which sources were used.

The 6,000 most-frequently-used English words included in these exercises are taken from A General Service List of English Words by Michael West (Longman, London 1953) and The Academic Word List by Coxhead (1998, 2000). We have also included more than 6,500 other words that we think well-educated children should know. These bonus words are in addition to those on the lists, making a total of more than 12,500 English words covered in the *Spelling Wisdom* series of books.

About Spelling Wisdom (cont.)

Index

The index in the back of each *Spelling Wisdom* book will give you a list of all the words included in that book's exercises. If you want to concentrate on or review a particular word, just look in the book's index to find any other exercises that use it. The index should also prove to be a friendly help if you spot a word or two in the child's written narrations that need some attention. You can easily find and assign a dictation exercise that uses the word in question and reinforces its correct spelling.

Spelling Variations

You may have noticed that the older writings contain some different spellings than we use today. For example, in Charlotte Mason's *Home Education* passage quoted at the beginning of this introduction, the word we spell today as "misspelled" was originally spelled "misspelt." Because the main objective of dictation is correct spelling, I updated such older words to modern spelling.

Two versions of the *Spelling Wisdom* series are available: American and British. The British version contains the British spelling preferences that I'm aware of. If I overlooked a possible alternate spelling, you can easily write your preferred spelling on the printed sheet that you give your student. (Then would you please e-mail me with the details of the change, or any other corrections, so I can change it in the book? Just send an e-mail to sonya@simplycharlottemason.com. Thank you!)

Poetry Variations

Many poets "take liberties" with word spellings in order to make the words fit in their assigned poetical places. Several of the poetry selections in these dictation exercises contained contracted words, such as "o'er" instead of "over." Since the goal of dictation is correct spelling, and missing letters don't help us reach that goal, I replaced contracted words with their spelled-out versions. You can easily enjoy the original form of the poems in your regular poetry studies, but for dictation purposes I thought the prudent path was to display the words correctly spelled.

Punctuation Variations

Because Charlotte advocated dictating "with a view to the pointing [punctuation], which the children are expected to put in as they write," I have attempted to edit the punctuation of the older passages to bring them more closely into conformity with modern punctuation guidelines. Encourage the children to make sure they are familiar with where the capital letters and punctuation marks go in their assigned exercises, even as they make sure they can spell all the words.

It is my hope that this collection of dictation exercises will make your journey more enjoyable and your path a little smoother on the "royal road to spelling."

(Quotations from *Home Education*, pp. 241, 242)

The Dictation Exercises

Motto for Students

By Charlotte Mason

I am;

I can;

I ought;

I will.

Exercise 2
A Proverb on Safety

Better be safe than sorry.

Exercise 3
A Proverb on Practice

Practice what you preach.

On Contentment
By Aesop

Be content with your lot; one cannot be first in everything.

The laborer is worthy of his hire.

Exercise 6
Happy Thought
By Robert Louis Stevenson

The world is so full of a number of things,
I'm sure we should all be as happy as kings.

Exercise 7
A Proverb on Perseverance

If at first you don't succeed, try, try again.

Exercise 8
On Sloth
By Benjamin Franklin

The sleeping fox catches no poultry. Up! Up!

A Proverb on Saving

A penny saved is a penny earned.

Exercise 10
Inferior Books
From *Oliver Twist* by Charles Dickens

There are books of which the backs and covers are by far the best parts.

Exercise 11
On Happiness
By Abraham Lincoln

Most folks are about as happy as they make up their minds to be.

Exercise 12
Rain
By Robert Louis Stevenson

The rain is raining all around,

It falls on field and tree,

It rains on the umbrellas here,

And on the ships at sea.

On Money
By Thomas Jefferson

Never spend your money before you have it.

Exercise 14
A Proverb on Starting

A trip of a thousand miles begins with one step.

Trust the Creator
By Ralph Waldo Emerson

All I have seen teaches me to trust the Creator for all I have not seen.

Exercise 16
Work with Serenity
By Ralph Waldo Emerson

The day is always his who works in it with serenity and great aims.

Early to Bed
By Benjamin Franklin

Early to bed and early to rise makes a man healthy, wealthy, and wise.

A Thought
By Robert Louis Stevenson

It is very nice to think

The world is full of meat and drink,

With little children saying grace

In every Christian kind of place.

On Books
By Ralph Waldo Emerson

Books are the best of things, well used; abused, among the worst.

Exercise 20
What I Must Do
By Ralph Waldo Emerson

What I must do is all that concerns me, not what the people think.

A Proverb on Marriage

Marry in haste; repent at leisure.

Great peace have they which love thy law, and nothing shall offend them.

An Enemy's Rake

From *The Deerslayer* by James Fenimore Cooper

Who is there that doesn't get a scratch when an enemy holds the rake?

Whole Duty of Children
By Robert Louis Stevenson

A child should always say what's true

And speak when he is spoken to,

And behave mannerly at table;

At least as far as he is able.

Boast not thyself of tomorrow, for thou knowest not what a day may bring forth.

Exercise 26
Variety Is the Spice of Life
By William Cowper

Variety is the very spice of life that gives it all its flavor.

Serpent Sting
From *Merchant of Venice* by Shakespeare

What! wouldst thou have a serpent sting thee twice?

Matthew 7:7

Ask, and it shall be given you; seek, and ye shall find; knock, and it shall be opened unto you.

The lip of truth shall be established forever, but a lying tongue is but for a moment.

Exercise 30
Daily Work
(Author Unknown)

Wash on Monday;

Iron on Tuesday;

Mend on Wednesday;

Churn on Thursday;

Clean on Friday;

Bake on Saturday;

Rest on Sunday.

On Observing

By Samuel Johnson

The world is not yet exhausted; let me see something tomorrow which I never saw before.

He that hath knowledge spareth his words, and a man of understanding is of an excellent spirit.

Exercise 33
On Time
By Benjamin Franklin

Dost thou love life? Then do not squander time, for that is the stuff life is made of.

As a jewel of gold in a swine's snout, so is a fair woman which is without discretion.

On Deception
By Sir Walter Scott

Oh what a tangled web we weave
when first we practice to deceive!

Bird Homes

If you watch carefully when you are out walking in the parks, fields, or woods, you will find that each family of birds builds a different kind of home.

He Prayeth Best
By Samuel Taylor Coleridge

He prayeth best who loveth best

All things both great and small;

For the dear God who loveth us,

He made and loveth all.

Books of Voyage

From *The Long Voyage* by Charles Dickens

When the wind is blowing and the sleet or rain is driving against the dark windows, I love to sit by the fire, thinking of what I have read in books of voyage and travel.

No Place Like Home
By John Howard Payne

Amid pleasures and palaces though we may roam,

Be it ever so humble, there's no place like home.

They Separated

From *The Pioneers* by James Fenimore Cooper

The Indian bent his head, and they separated—the one to seek his hut and the other to join his party at the supper table.

A Proverb on Details

For want of a nail the shoe was lost; for want of a shoe the horse was lost; and for want of a horse the rider was lost.

Gaily-Dressed Holiday Folks
From *The Shoes of Fortune* by Hans Christian Andersen

It was noon; and the weather, that had threatened rain, began to clear up, while gaily-dressed holiday folks filled the streets.

Exercise 43
We Thank Thee
(Author Unknown)

For mother-love and father-care,

For brothers strong and sisters fair,

For love at home and here each day,

For guidance lest we go astray,

Father in Heaven, we thank Thee.

For this new morning with its light,

For rest and shelter of the night,

For health and food, for love and friends,

For everything His goodness sends,

Father in Heaven, we thank Thee.

Every New Year
By Benjamin Franklin

Be at war with your vices,

At peace with your neighbors,

And let every New Year find you a better man.

March Days
From *Great Expectations* by Charles Dickens

It was one of those March days when the sun shines hot and the wind blows cold, when it is summer in the light and winter in the shade.

Exercise 46
Luke 12:27

Consider the lilies, how they grow: they toil not, they spin not; and yet I say unto you that Solomon in all his glory was not arrayed like one of these.

Too Powerful for Speech
From *The Pioneers* by James Fenimore Cooper

The transition from excitement to disappointment was too powerful for speech; and even Richard lost the use of an organ that was seldom known to fail him.

Exercise 48
Houses

Did you ever notice how many kinds of houses you pass? Some of them are large; others are small. Perhaps some of them are made of wood or brick. Of what other things can people make houses?

Thirty Days Hath September
(Author Unknown)

Thirty days hath September,

April, June, and November;

All the rest have thirty-one,

Excepting February alone,

Which has only eight and a score

Till leap year gives it one day more.

What Are You Driving At?

From *The Adventures of Sherlock Holmes* by Sir Arthur Conan Doyle

---

To my surprise the question provoked a burst of anger from the salesman.
"Now, then, mister," said he with his head cocked and his arms akimbo,
"what are you driving at? Let's have it straight, now."

Stars

Every clear night you can see many beautiful stars in the sky. Do you ever look at them and talk about them? I hope you do. And I hope you know the names of some of the stars.

Do, In Place of Talking

From *The Deerslayer* by James Fenimore Cooper

"At any rate, we know you can use a paddle, young man," said Hutter, "and that's all we shall ask of you tonight. Let us waste no more time, but get into the canoe and do, in place of talking."

The Dock-Leaf

From *The Happy Family* by Hans Christian Andersen

Really, the largest green leaf in this country is a dock-leaf. If one holds it before one, it is like a whole apron, and if one holds it over one's head in rainy weather, it is almost as good as an umbrella, for it is so immensely large.

Exercise 54
In Intense Darkness
From *The Deerslayer* by James Fenimore Cooper

The intense darkness that prevailed so close in with the forest, too, served as an effectual screen, and so long as care was had not to make a noise, there was little or no danger of being detected.

Cradle Hymn
By Martin Luther

Away in a manger no crib for a bed;

The little Lord Jesus lay down His sweet head.

The stars in the night sky looked down where He lay;

The little Lord Jesus asleep on the hay.

The cattle are lowing, the baby awakes;

But little Lord Jesus no crying He makes.

I love Thee, Lord Jesus, look down from the sky;

And stay by my cradle till morning is nigh.

Baby Squirrels

Mother Squirrel had four baby squirrels. Their home was a soft nest in a hollow tree. At first the squirrels were ugly little things. They had big heads, no fur, and their eyes were shut tight. By and by the little eyes opened, and the fur grew fast. Soon it was as smooth as satin.

Mark 12:30, 31

And thou shalt love the Lord thy God with all thy heart and with all thy soul and with all thy mind and with all thy strength; this is the first commandment. And the second is like, namely this: Thou shalt love thy neighbor as thyself. There is none other commandment greater than these.

Giving Over These Things

From *Robinson Crusoe* by Daniel DeFoe

Having now brought my mind a little to relish my condition, and given over looking out to sea to see if I could spy a ship—I say, giving over these things—I began to apply myself to arrange my way of living and to make things as easy to me as I could.

Pray, Be Precise
From *The Adventures of Sherlock Holmes* by Sir Arthur Conan Doyle

---

Sherlock Holmes had been leaning back in his chair with his eyes closed and his head sunk in a cushion, but he half opened his lids now and glanced across at his visitor.

"Pray, be precise as to details," said he.

Dick's Taxi Ride

Dick bounced off the rug on the floor of the taxi as it squealed to a stop behind a bus at the traffic light. His suitcase popped open and spit out a stocking with a stripe and a hole in one toe. Dick stuffed the stocking back in the suitcase as the motor roared into life and the taxi lurched onwards.

The Vowels: An Enigma
By Jonathan Swift

We are little airy creatures,

All of different voice and features;

One of us in glass is set,

One of us you'll find in jet,

The other you may see in tin,

And the fourth a box within;

If the fifth you should pursue,

It can never fly from you.

Exercise 62
Prejudice
From *The Life of Jesus Christ for the Young* by Richard Newton

___

The word "prejudice" is made up of two Latin words. One of these means "to judge," or "to form an opinion," or "to make up our minds on any subject"; and the other means "beforehand." And a person who has a prejudice is one who has made up his mind about something before he understands it.

Busy As Water

From *Swinton's Advanced Fourth Reader*

Is there anything in the world more busy and active than water, as it rushes along in the swift brook, or dashes over the stones, or spouts up in the fountain, or trickles down from the roof, or shakes itself into ripples on the surface of the pond as the wind blows over it?

Exercise 64
Searching for Mom

Jan peeked into the open door of her parents' bathroom to see if Mom was in there. On the counter was a bottle of nail polish, a comb, a towel, and the razor her dad used to shave with. On the floor was one lone sock that had fallen out of the laundry basket. Jan picked up the sock and went to look for her mother elsewhere.

Respected By All
From *Treasure Island* by Robert Louis Stevenson

All the crew respected and even obeyed him. He had a way of talking to each and doing everybody some particular service. To me he was unweariedly kind and always glad to see me in the galley, which he kept as clean as a new pin, the dishes hanging up burnished and his parrot in a cage in one corner.

The Little Boat
From *The Wind in the Willows* by Kenneth Grahame

The Rat said nothing but stooped and unfastened a rope and hauled on it, then lightly stepped into a little boat which the Mole had not observed. It was painted blue outside and white within, and was just the size for two animals; and the Mole's whole heart went out to it at once, even though he did not yet fully understand its uses.

Pippa's Song
By Robert Browning

The year's at the spring,

And day's at the morn;

Morning's at seven;

The hillside's dew-pearled;

The lark's on the wing;

The snail's on the thorn;

God's in His Heaven—

All's right with the world!

The Industrious Spider
From *Friends and Helpers* by Sarah J. Eddy

The spider is one of the most industrious, clean, and patient workers in the world. More than six hundred separate strands go to make one slender thread of her web. She can choose, moreover, whether she will spin a fine or coarse, a dry or spangled thread for the particular work she has in hand.

The Clothes Are Ready
From *The Emperor's New Clothes* by Hans Christian Andersen

The rogues sat up the whole of the night before the day on which the procession was to take place, and had sixteen lights burning, so that everyone might see how anxious they were to finish the Emperor's new suit. They pretended to roll the cloth off the looms, cut the air with their scissors, and sewed with needles without any thread in them. "See!" cried they, at last. "The Emperor's new clothes are ready!"

Average Speed
From *Amusements in Mathematics* by Henry Ernest Dudeney

In a recent motor ride it was found that we had gone at the rate of ten miles an hour, but we did the return journey over the same route, owing to the roads being more clear of traffic, at fifteen miles an hour. What was our average speed? Do not be too hasty in your answer to this simple little question or it is pretty certain that you will be wrong.

The Fisher and the Fish
By Aesop

It happened that a Fisher, after fishing all day, caught only a little fish. "Pray, let me go, master," said the Fish. "I am much too small for your eating just now. If you put me back into the river I shall soon grow, then you can make a fine meal off me."

"Nay, nay, my little Fish," said the Fisher, "I have you now. I may not catch you hereafter."

After Their Kind

From *Swinton's Advanced Fourth Reader*

Each plant will grow according to its own seed. The seed of a turnip will begin to grow with one cell and then make cell after cell, with all the cells packed pretty close together. But all these cells will grow together in such a way as to make a turnip plant. An acorn will grow in the same way, but all its cells will grow together in such a way as to make an oak tree.

My Heart Leaps Up When I Behold
By William Wordsworth

My heart leaps up when I behold

A rainbow in the sky:

So was it when my life began,

So is it now I am a man,

So be it when I shall grow old

Or let me die!

The Child is father of the Man:

And I could wish my days to be

Bound each to each by natural piety.

Exercise 74
Silver's Scheme
From *Treasure Island* by Robert Louis Stevenson

It was no wonder the men were in a good humor now. For my part, I was horribly cast down. Should the scheme he had now sketched prove feasible, Silver, already doubly a traitor, would not hesitate to adopt it. He had still a foot in either camp, and there was no doubt he would prefer wealth and freedom with the pirates to a bare escape from hanging, which was the best he had to hope on our side.

What Is the Time?

From *Amusements in Mathematics* by Henry Ernest Dudeney

"I say, Rackbrane, what is the time?" an acquaintance asked our friend the professor the other day. The answer was certainly curious.

"If you add one quarter of the time from noon till now to half the time from now till noon tomorrow, you will get the time exactly."

What was the time of day when the professor spoke?

The Beautiful Cake

From *Five Little Peppers and How They Grew* by Margaret Sidney

Oh, dear, of all things in the world! The beautiful cake over which so many hopes had been formed, that was to have given so much happiness on the morrow to the dear mother, presented a forlorn appearance as it stood there in anything but holiday attire. It was quite black on the top, in the center of which was a depressing little dump, as if to say, "My feelings wouldn't allow me to rise to the occasion."

A Note from Jeff

Mom,

Cousin Ann just called on the telephone to inform us that she has a cough and all her muscles ache. I thought she might have the flu, but she wanted to argue with me. She is sure she has a rare disease and needs to go to the hospital right away. Please call her.

Jeff

In Springtime
From *Swinton's Advanced Fourth Reader*

In springtime the sweet odors from budding plants remind us of the flowers that soon shall open to our gaze their manifold beauties of form and color. Our gardens will soon be full of purest white, of red, of yellow, and of blue. Orange and purple, too, of matchless tint will be seen in many flowers, and green of course will not be wanting.

Wind and the Leaves
(Author Unknown)

"Come, little Leaves," said the Wind one day,

"Come over the meadows with me and play;

Put on your dresses of red and gold;

Summer is gone, and the days grow cold."

Soon as the Leaves heard the Wind's loud call,

Down they came fluttering, one and all;

Over the fields they danced and flew,

Singing the soft little songs they knew.

Dancing and whirling the little Leaves went;

Winter had called them, and they were content.

Soon, fast asleep in their earthy beds,

The snow laid a coverlet over their heads.

Exercise 80
A Saucer of Milk

From *The Adventures of Sherlock Holmes* by Sir Arthur Conan Doyle

---

"Well, look at this!" He took up a small saucer of milk which stood on the top of it.

"No; we don't keep a cat. But there is a cheetah and a baboon."

"Ah, yes, of course! Well, a cheetah is just a big cat, and yet a saucer of milk does not go very far in satisfying its wants, I daresay."

A Quart or a Liter

"I'm so thirsty I could drink a quart of water," panted Evelyn.

"Well, I'm so thirsty I could drink a liter," replied Davie.

Evelyn paused and wrinkled her brow in thought. "Which is bigger: a quart or a liter?" she asked.

"I'm not sure," Davie admitted. Then he added proudly, "But I do know they're both bigger than a milliliter!"

Brownie Beaver

Brownie Beaver, like all beavers, could do many things that other forest people are not able to do at all. Cutting down a tree is one of the things that only a beaver can do.

When Brownie Beaver saw a tree he wanted to cut down, he set to work at once. He did not even go home to get any tools. There was no need to do this. He always had his tools with him. For strange as it may seem, he used his teeth to do his wood-cutting.

The Dog's Reflection
By Aesop

It happened that a dog had got a piece of meat and was carrying it home in his mouth to eat it in peace. Now on his way home, he had to cross a plank lying across a running brook. As he crossed, he looked down and saw his own shadow reflected in the water beneath. Thinking it was another dog with another piece of meat, he made up his mind to have that also. So he made a snap at the shadow in the water, but as he opened his mouth, the piece of meat fell out, dropped into the water, and was never seen more.

Take Time By the Forelock
From *Treasure Island* by Robert Louis Stevenson

"First point," began Mr. Smollett. "We must go on, because we can't turn back. If I gave the word to go about, they would rise at once. Second point, we have time before us—at least until this treasure is found. Third point, there are faithful hands. Now, sir, it's got to come to blows sooner or later, and what I propose is to take time by the forelock, as the saying is, and come to blows some fine day when they least expect it."

The Lamb
By William Blake

Little lamb, who made thee?
Dost thou know who made thee?
Gave thee life, and bid thee feed
By the stream and over the mead;
Gave thee clothing of delight,
Softest clothing, woolly, bright;
Gave thee such a tender voice,
Making all the vales rejoice?
Little lamb, who made thee?
Dost thou know who made thee?

Little lamb, I'll tell thee,
Little lamb, I'll tell thee:
He is called by thy name,
For He calls Himself a Lamb.
He is meek, and He is mild;
He became a little child.
I a child, and thou a lamb,
We are called by His name.
Little lamb, God bless thee;
Little lamb, God bless thee.

A Young Seed
From *Swinton's Advanced Fourth Reader*

When a young seed begins to grow, it starts with one little cell. This cell is a kind of round bag, or tiny bladder. It is hollow and has in it a sort of jelly.

Those who study plants can with their microscopes watch just how the young seed grows. When first they observe the tiny sac, or cell, it is not larger than the point of a pin. They can see it grow larger, but even when it is full-grown it is not larger than the dot over this letter i.

A Breathing Spell
From *Five Little Peppers and How They Grew* by Margaret Sidney

The little old kitchen had quieted down from the bustle and confusion of mid-day; and now, with its afternoon manners on, presented a holiday aspect that as the principal room in the brown house, it was eminently proper it should have. It was just on the edge of the twilight; and the little Peppers, all except Ben, the oldest of the flock, were enjoying a "breathing spell," as their mother called it, which meant some quiet work suitable for the hour.

The Dog in the Manger
By Aesop

A dog, looking out for its afternoon nap, jumped into the manger of an ox and lay there cozily upon the straw. But soon the ox, returning from its afternoon walk, came up to the manger and wanted to eat some of the straw. The dog in rage, being awakened from its slumber, stood up and barked at the ox, and whenever it came near, attempted to bite it. At last the ox had to give up the hope of getting at the straw and went away muttering, "Ah, people often grudge others what they cannot enjoy themselves."

First Place I Remember

From *Black Beauty* by Anna Sewell

The first place that I can well remember was a large pleasant meadow with a pond of clear water in it. Some shady trees leaned over it, and rushes and water lilies grew at the deep end. Over the hedge on one side, we looked into a plowed field, and on the other, we looked over a gate at our master's house, which stood by the roadside; at the top of the meadow was a grove of fir trees and at the bottom, a running brook overhung by a steep bank.

Exercise 90
Packing the Basket
From *The Wind in the Willows* by Kenneth Grahame

Packing the basket was not quite such pleasant work as unpacking the basket. It never is. But the Mole was bent on enjoying everything, and although just when he had got the basket packed and strapped up tightly, he saw a plate staring up at him from the grass, and when the job had been done again, the Rat pointed out a fork which anybody ought to have seen, and last of all, behold! the mustard pot, which he had been sitting on without knowing it—still, somehow, the thing got finished at last without much loss of temper.

Psalm 100

Make a joyful noise unto the Lord, all ye lands.

Serve the Lord with gladness:

come before his presence with singing.

Know ye that the Lord he is God:

it is he that hath made us, and not we ourselves;

we are his people, and the sheep of his pasture.

Enter into his gates with thanksgiving,

and into his courts with praise:

be thankful unto him, and bless his name.

For the Lord is good; his mercy is everlasting;

and his truth endureth to all generations.

Ocean Depths
From *The Life of Jesus Christ for the Young* by Richard Newton

---

In sailing across the ocean, if we attempt to measure the depth of the water in different places, we shall find that it varies very much. There are hardly two places in which it is exactly the same. In some places, it is easy enough to find the bottom. In others, it is necessary to lengthen the line greatly before it can be reached. And then there are other places where the water is so deep that the longest line, ordinarily used, cannot reach to the bottom. We know that there is a bottom, but it is very hard to get down to it.

Exercise 93
Brother and Sister
From *Five Little Peppers and How They Grew* by Margaret Sidney

"To help mother" was the great ambition of all the children, older and younger; but in Polly's and Ben's souls the desire grew so overwhelmingly great as to absorb all lesser thoughts. Many and vast were their secret plans by which they were to astonish her at some future day, which they would only confide—as they did everything else—to one another. For this brother and sister were everything to each other and stood loyally together through "thick and thin."

Exercise 94
Sour Grapes
By Aesop

On a hot summer's day, a fox was strolling through an orchard till he came to a bunch of grapes just ripening on a vine, which had been trained over a lofty branch. "Just the thing to quench my thirst," said he. Drawing back a few paces, he took a run and a jump, and just missed the branch. Turning round again with a One, Two, Three, he jumped up, but with no greater success. Again and again he tried after the tempting morsel, but at last had to give up, and walked away with his nose in the air, saying, "I am sure they are sour."

The Intelligence of Rats
From *Friends and Helpers* by Sarah J. Eddy

The intelligence shown by rats is remarkable. They have frequently been known to carry eggs up and down stairs in their paws, one rat pushing the egg and others receiving it. It happened one day, that a trap was set and carefully watched. A young rat was about to step upon the fatal spring when the watcher saw an old rat rush to the rescue. The little one was seized by the tail and promptly dragged off to his hole. Probably he was told to be less reckless in the future.

On the Swing
From *The Snow Queen* by Hans Christian Andersen

Between the trees a long board is hanging; it is a swing. Two little girls are sitting in it and swing themselves backwards and forwards; their frocks are as white as snow, and long green silk ribbons flutter from their bonnets. Their brother, who is older than they are, stands up in the swing; he twines his arms round the cords to hold himself fast, for in one hand he has a little cup and in the other, a clay pipe. He is blowing soap bubbles.

The Shepherd's Song
By John Bunyan

He that is down needs fear no fall,

He that is low, no pride;

He that is humble ever shall

Have God to be his guide.

I am content with what I have,

Little be it or much:

And, Lord, contentment still I crave,

Because Thou savest such.

Fullness to such a burden is

That go on pilgrimage:

Here little, and hereafter bliss,

Is best from age to age.

Exercise 98
Polly Was Homesick
From *Five Little Peppers and How They Grew* by Margaret Sidney

Yes, it must be confessed. Polly was homesick. All her imaginations of her mother's hard work, increased by her absence, loomed up before her, till she was almost ready to fly home without a minute's warning. At night, when no one knew it, the tears would come racing over the poor, forlorn little face and would not be squeezed back. It got to be noticed finally; and one and all redoubled their exertions to make everything twice as pleasant as ever!

Now the Tree did not even dare tremble. What a state he was in! He was so uneasy lest he should lose something of his splendor, that he was quite bewildered amidst the glare and brightness; when suddenly both folding-doors opened and a troop of children rushed in as if they would upset the Tree. The older persons followed quietly; the little ones stood quite still. But it was only for a moment; then they shouted that the whole place re-echoed with their rejoicing; they danced round the Tree, and one present after the other was pulled off.

Garden Tools

From *The Secret Garden* by Frances Hodgson Burnett

They went from bush to bush and from tree to tree. He was very strong and clever with his knife and knew how to cut the dry and dead wood away, and could tell when an unpromising bough or twig had still green life in it. In the course of half an hour Mary thought she could tell too, and when he cut through a lifeless-looking branch she would cry out joyfully under her breath when she caught sight of the least shade of moist green. The spade and hoe and fork were very useful. He showed her how to use the fork while he dug about roots with the spade and stirred the earth and let the air in.

Exercise 101
The Squash
From *Little Women* by Louisa May Alcott

Once upon a time a farmer planted a little seed in his garden, and after a while it sprouted and became a vine and bore many squashes. One day in October, when they were ripe, he picked one and took it to market. A grocerman bought and put it in his shop. That same morning, a little girl in a brown hat and blue dress, with a round face and snub nose, went and bought it for her mother. She lugged it home, cut it up, and boiled it in the big pot, then mashed some of it with salt and butter for dinner. And to the rest she added a pint of milk, two eggs, four spoons of sugar, nutmeg, and some crackers, put it in a deep dish, and baked it till it was brown and nice, and next day it was eaten by a family named March.

                    www.SimplyCharlotteMason.com

Catching Butterflies
From *Friends and Helpers* by Sarah J. Eddy

To some people, catching butterflies seems a harmless sport, especially if the pretty creature is soon released and allowed to flutter away in the sunshine. Those who have studied them, however, say that much suffering is caused in this way.

On the surface of the wing are soft, tiny feathers, set row upon row like shingles on a house. There are over two million feathers on each wing. When the butterfly is held in hot, hasty hands, these feathers are rubbed off and do not grow again.

The Arrow and the Song
By Henry Wadsworth Longfellow

I shot an arrow into the air,

It fell to earth, I knew not where;

For, so swiftly it flew, the sight

Could not follow it in its flight.

I breathed a song into the air,

It fell to earth, I knew not where;

For who has sight so keen and strong,

That it can follow the flight of song?

Long, long afterward, in an oak

I found the arrow, still unbroke;

And the song, from beginning to end,

I found again in the heart of a friend.

The Captain's Clothes
From *Treasure Island* by Robert Louis Stevenson

All the time he lived with us, the captain made no change whatever in his dress but to buy some stockings from a hawker. One of the cocks of his hat having fallen down, he let it hang from that day forth, though it was a great annoyance when it blew. I remember the appearance of his coat, which he patched himself upstairs in his room, and which, before the end, was nothing but patches. He never wrote or received a letter, and he never spoke with any but the neighbors and with these, for the most part, only when drunk on rum. The great sea-chest none of us had ever seen open.

The Cat Family
From *Friends and Helpers* by Sarah J. Eddy

Our little house cat belongs to the same family as the lion, the tiger, and the leopard. They are known as the old and powerful family of cats, and though pussy is small, tame, and gentle, she is not unlike her fierce cousins in many of her ways.

All cats have sharp claws which can be drawn back until quite out of sight. They walk softly because their feet are padded with soft, elastic cushions. Not only is a cat one of the most sure-footed animals in the world, but she is also one of the most graceful.

Exercise 106
Tell a Story
From *The Elderbush* by Hans Christian Andersen

Said the old man, "I ought now to tell you a story, but I don't know any more."

"You can make one in a moment," said the little boy. "My mother says that all you look at can be turned into a fairy tale and that you can find a story in everything."

"Yes, but such tales and stories are good for nothing. The right sort come of themselves; they tap at my forehead and say, 'Here we are.'"

"Won't there be a tap soon?" asked the little boy. And his mother laughed, put some Elder-flowers in the teapot, and poured boiling water upon them.

Reddy Fox

From *The Burgess Animal Book for Children* by Thornton W. Burgess

"Reddy Fox hunts with ears, eyes, and nose," continued Peter. "Many a time I've watched him listening for the squeak of Danny Meadow Mouse or watching for the grass to move and show where Danny was hiding; and many a time he has found my scent with his wonderful nose and followed me just as Bowser the Hound follows him. I guess there isn't much going on that Reddy's eyes, ears, and nose don't tell him. But it is Reddy's quick wits that the rest of us fear most. We never know what new trick he will try. Lots of enemies are easy to fool, but Reddy isn't one of them. Sometimes I think he knows more about me than I know about myself. I guess it is just pure luck that he hasn't caught me with some of those smart tricks of his."

Direction
From *Home Geography for Primary Grades*

The way to a place is called "direction." In order to find a place, we must know in what direction from us it lies, and we have names for directions, such as north, south, east, and west. We may know these directions by seeing where the sun is.

The sun seems to rise toward the east and set toward the west. The west is just the opposite direction from the east.

When your right hand is pointing to the east and your left hand to the west, your face is toward the north and your back is toward the south.

Bed in Summer
By Robert Louis Stevenson

In winter I get up at night
And dress by yellow candlelight.
In summer, quite the other way,
I have to go to bed by day.

I have to go to bed and see
The birds still hopping on the tree,
Or hear the grown-up people's feet
Still going past me in the street.

And does it not seem hard to you,
When all the sky is clear and blue,
And I should like so much to play,
To have to go to bed by day?

Checking on the Weavers
From *The Emperor's New Clothes* by Hans Christian Andersen

"I should like to know how the weavers are getting on with my cloth," said the Emperor to himself after some little time had elapsed; he was, however, rather embarrassed when he remembered that a simpleton, or one unfit for his office, would be unable to see the manufacture. To be sure, he thought he had nothing to risk in his own person; but yet, he would prefer sending somebody else to bring him intelligence about the weavers and their work before he troubled himself in the affair. All the people throughout the city had heard of the wonderful property the cloth was to possess; and all were anxious to learn how wise, or how ignorant, their neighbors might prove to be.

Mr. Brown's Word
From "Honor and Duty" by Laura Ingalls Wilder

"Now can we depend on you in this?" asked Mr. Jones.

"Certainly you can," replied Mr. Brown. "I'll do it!"

"But you failed us before, you know," continued Mr. Jones, "and it made us a lot of trouble. How would it be for you to put up a forfeit? Will you put up some money as security that you will not fail; will you bet on it?"

"No-o-o," answered Mr. Brown. "I won't bet on it, but I'll give you my word of honor."

How much was Mr. Brown's word worth? I would not want to risk much on it. Would you?

Exercise 112
Winsome Bluebird
From *Mother West Wind "When" Stories* by Thornton W. Burgess

Of all the joyous sounds of all the year, there is none more loved by Peter
Rabbit, and the rest of us for that matter, than the soft whistle of Winsome
Bluebird in the spring. The first time Peter hears it, he always jumps up in the
air, kicks his long heels together, and does a funny little dance of pure joy, for
he knows that Winsome Bluebird is the herald of sweet Mistress Spring and that
she is not far behind him. It is the end of the shivery, sad time and the beginning
of the happy, glad time, and Peter rejoices when he hears that sweet, soft voice
which is sometimes so hard to locate, seeming to come from everywhere and
nowhere.

Psalm 23

The Lord is my shepherd; I shall not want.

He maketh me to lie down in green pastures:

he leadeth me beside the still waters.

He restoreth my soul:

he leadeth me in the paths of righteousness for his name's sake.

Yea, though I walk through the valley of the shadow of death,

I will fear no evil: for thou art with me;

thy rod and thy staff they comfort me.

Thou preparest a table before me

in the presence of mine enemies:

thou anointest my head with oil;

my cup runneth over.

Surely goodness and mercy shall follow me all the days of my life:

and I will dwell in the house of the Lord for ever.

Exercise 114
Underwater Plants
From *Mother West Wind "When" Stories* by Thornton W. Burgess

Peter Rabbit had taken it into his funny little head to wander down the Laughing Brook to below the Smiling Pool. It was open there, and in one place the bank was quite high and steep. Peter sat down on the edge of it and looked down. Right under him the Laughing Brook was very quiet and clear. Peter sat gazing down into it. He could see all the pebbles on the bottom and queer little plants growing among them. It seemed very queer, very queer indeed to Peter that plants, real plants, could be growing down there under water. Somehow he couldn't make it seem right that anything but fish should be able to live down there.

Cotton
From *Home Geography for Primary Grades*

Did you ever see a field of cotton? In the summer the young plant is covered with pretty, pale yellow flowers. In the autumn you see the pod or boll, which contains the cotton.

As the pod ripens, it bursts open. The cotton field is now a pretty sight—the bright green leaves, yellow blossoms, and snowy cotton all mingled together. Form a picture in your mind of a field of cotton in bloom.

The cotton is now picked. The first thing is to separate it from its seed. This is done by a machine called a cotton gin.

Now it is ready to be pressed in great bales and sent to market. It will, at last, go to the cotton mills and be spun into thread, then woven into muslin, calico, etc.

Linen
From *Home Geography for Primary Grades*

There is another plant from which clothing is made.

Do you know what plant linen is made from? Linen comes from the flax plant.

Flax is a small plant which grows two or three feet high, bearing on the top a bunch of pretty blue flowers. A field of flax in bloom is a very pretty sight.

The flax does not grow in a pod like cotton. The stalk of the plant is covered with a bark, or skin, containing fibers. These fibers are spun into thread, which is woven into a cloth called linen.

The Ant

By Oliver Herford

My child, observe the useful Ant,

How hard she works each day;

She works as hard as adamant

(That's very hard, they say.)

She has no time to gallivant;

She has no time to play.

Let Fido chase his tail all day;

Let Kitty play at tag;

She has no time to throw away,

She has no tail to wag;

She hurries round from morn till night;

She never, never sleeps;

She seizes everything in sight,

She drags it home with all her might,

And all she takes she keeps.

To every thing there is a season, and a time to every purpose under the heaven:

A time to be born, and a time to die;

A time to plant, and a time to pluck up that which is planted;

A time to kill, and a time to heal;

A time to break down, and a time to build up;

A time to weep, and a time to laugh;

A time to mourn, and a time to dance;

A time to cast away stones, and a time to gather stones together;

A time to embrace, and a time to refrain from embracing;

A time to get, and a time to lose;

A time to keep, and a time to cast away;

A time to rend, and a time to sew;

A time to keep silence, and a time to speak;

A time to love, and a time to hate;

A time of war, and a time of peace.

The Ant and the Grasshopper
By Aesop

In a field one summer's day, a grasshopper was hopping about, chirping and singing to its heart's content. An ant passed by, bearing along with great toil an ear of corn he was taking to the nest.

"Why not come and chat with me," said the grasshopper, "instead of toiling and moiling in that way?"

"I am helping to lay up food for the winter," said the ant, "and recommend you to do the same."

"Why bother about winter?" said the grasshopper. "We have plenty of food at present." But the ant went on its way and continued its toil.

When the winter came, the grasshopper had no food and found itself dying of hunger, while it saw the ants distributing every day corn and grain from the stores they had collected in the summer. Then the grasshopper knew: It is best to prepare for the days of necessity.

Breaking In
From *Black Beauty* by Anna Sewell

Every one may not know what breaking in is, therefore I will describe it. It means to teach a horse to wear a saddle and bridle and to carry on his back a man, woman, or child; to go just the way they wish and to go quietly. Besides this, he has to learn to wear a collar, a crupper, and a breeching and to stand still while they are put on; then to have a cart or a chaise fixed behind, so that he cannot walk or trot without dragging it after him; and he must go fast or slow, just as his driver wishes. He must never start at what he sees, nor speak to other horses, nor bite, nor kick, nor have any will of his own; but always do his master's will, even though he may be very tired or hungry; but the worst of all is, when his harness is once on, he may neither jump for joy nor lie down for weariness. So you see, this breaking in is a great thing.

The North Star
From *Home Geography for Primary Grades*

You have learned how to tell north, south, east, and west by the sun; but how can we tell these directions at night?

Look for a group of seven bright stars in the north part of the sky. Some people think that this group of stars looks like a wagon and three horses; others say that it looks like a plow.

The proper name of the group containing these seven stars is the Great Bear. The group was given this name because men at first thought it looked like a bear with a long tail.

These seven stars are called the Dipper. It is a part of a larger group called the Great Bear. Find the two bright twinkling stars farthest from its handle. A line drawn through them will point to another star, not quite so bright, called the North Star. That star is always in the north; so by it, on a clear night, you can tell the other directions at once.

Sailors out on the sea at night often find direction by looking at the North Star.

A Compass
From *Home Geography for Primary Grades*

But there are times when it is cloudy and neither the sun nor the stars can be seen. How can we tell direction then?

Have you ever seen a compass? It is a box in which is a little needle swinging on the top of a pin. When this needle is at rest, one end of it points to the north.

As the needle shows where the north is, it is easy to find the south, the east, or the west.

With the compass as a guide, the sailor, in the darkest night, can tell in what direction he is going.

North, south, east, and west are called the chief points of the compass.

Other directions are northeast, halfway between north and east; northwest, halfway between north and west; southeast, halfway between south and east; and southwest, halfway between south and west.

Exercise 123
Distance
From *Home Geography for Primary Grades*

To tell where a place is, we must know its direction. But this is not all; we must also know how far it is from us; that is, its distance. To find this out, we measure.

You have often heard of an inch, a foot, and a yard. Your ruler is twelve inches long; that is, a foot. Three lengths of your ruler make a yard. A yardstick is three feet long.

With these measures you can tell how long your book or your desk is, or how long and wide the room is.

The inch, foot, and yard are used for measuring short distances. But when we wish to tell the distance between objects far apart, we use another measure called a mile. A mile is much longer than a yard.

Think of some object that is a mile from your house. How long would it take you to walk that distance?

Exercise 124
The Owl
By Alfred, Lord Tennyson

When cats run home and light is come,

And dew is cold upon the ground,

And the far-off stream is dumb,

And the whirring sail goes round,

And the whirring sail goes round;

Alone and warming his five wits,

The white owl in the belfry sits.

When merry milkmaids click the latch,

And rarely smells the new-mown hay,

And the cock hath sung beneath the thatch

Twice or thrice his roundelay,

Twice or thrice his roundelay;

Alone and warming his five wits,

The white owl in the belfry sits.

Exercise 125
Miner the Mole
From *The Burgess Animal Book for Children* by Thornton W. Burgess

Peter chuckled. "Now isn't that funny?" he demanded of no one at all, for he was quite alone. Then he answered himself. "It certainly is," said he. "Here I am on my way to learn something about Miner the Mole, and I trip over one of the queer little ridges he is forever making. It wasn't here yesterday, so that means that he is at work right around here now. Hello, I thought so!"

Peter had been looking along that little ridge and had discovered that it ended only a short distance from him. Now as he looked at it again, he saw the flat surface of the ground at the end of the ridge rise as if being pushed up from beneath, and that little ridge became just so much longer. Peter understood perfectly. Out of sight, beneath the surface, Miner the Mole was at work. He was digging a tunnel, and that ridge was simply the roof to that tunnel. It was so near the surface of the ground that Miner simply pushed up the loose soil as he bored his way along, and this made the little ridge over which Peter had stumbled.

Mannheim, Nov. 5, 1777

My dear Coz—Buzz,

I have safely received your precious epistle—thistle, and from it I perceive—achieve, that my aunt—gaunt, and you—shoe, are quite well—bell. I have today a letter—setter, from my papa—ah-ha, safe in my hands—sands. I hope you also got—trot, my Mannheim letter—setter. Now for a little sense—pence. The prelate's seizure—leisure, grieves me much—touch, but he will, I hope, get well—sell. You write—blight, you will keep—cheap, your promise to write to me—he-he, to Augsburg soon—spoon. Well, I shall be very glad—mad. You further write, indeed you declare, you pretend, you hint, you vow, you explain, you distinctly say, you long, you wish, you desire, you choose, command, and point out, you let me know and inform me that I must send you my portrait soon—moon. Eh, bien! you shall have it before long—song. Now I wish you good night—tight.

Exercise 127
Water Vapor
From *Home Geography for Primary Grades*

What happens when a kettle of water is put on a hot stove? The water gets hot and boils away.

Where does it go? Is it destroyed? The water is changed, but it is not destroyed. Coal burns, but we do not get rid of it altogether. It is changed into gas and smoke and ashes.

What is the water changed into? It is changed to vapor. If we let the kettle remain on the fire long enough, the water it contains will all pass away as vapor.

Where does the vapor go? The water, though turned into vapor, must be somewhere. It is floating about in the air of the room, though we cannot see it. The air holds the vapor, just as a sponge holds water.

Exercise 128
Dew
From *Home Geography for Primary Grades*

The sun is all the time heating the water on the land and in the sea, and changing it into vapor, which rises in the air. We cannot see the vapor, but it is in the air around us.

If the vapor in the air is suddenly cooled, a strange thing happens. Some of it quickly changes back into water. You have often seen, in the early morning, little drops of water hanging like pearls upon the blades of grass.

Now, where do these drops come from? They come from the air. The vapor in the air floats against the cold grass and leaves, and is cooled and changed into tiny drops of water. We call this dew.

Clouds
From *Home Geography for Primary Grades*

When vapor rises high in the cool air, it is turned into very small drops of water or minute crystals of ice, and we can see it floating about in the air. It is then called a cloud. Almost any clear day you may see clouds form and then seem to melt away.

You have seen on a blue sky, light, fleecy feather-clouds. They are very high up, and it is very cold where they are. You have also noticed the clouds at sunset with their beautiful colors. As the sun sank lower and lower, how did they change in shape and color?

When clouds are low down, near the earth, we call them fog or mist.

If clouds are cooled, the little particles of water gather into large drops and fall as rain. If the drops should freeze in falling, we would call them hail.

Sometimes, when it is very cold, the moisture in the air freezes before it forms into drops, and falls in the beautiful flakes we call snow.

As vapor rises into high, cool air, or is carried with the air in winds up the sides of mountains, it turns into water again and comes falling down as rain.

Now think where the rain that falls on mountains must go. Some of the water runs off on the surface, down the mountain slope. Some sinks into the ground and runs along in little streams below the surface. It will appear again, bubbling out of the mountainside as a spring. The spring is the beginning of a river.

From the spring flows a tiny, thread-like stream, so small that we can easily step across it. This little stream is called a rill.

Other rills meet this and form a larger stream, which is called a brook or creek.

As the brook flows on, it is joined by other streams, until, little by little, it becomes a wide and deep river on which large boats may float. At last, it finds its way into the ocean.

Blessed is the man

that walketh not in the counsel of the ungodly,

nor standeth in the way of sinners,

nor sitteth in the seat of the scornful.

But his delight is in the law of the Lord;

and in his law doth he meditate day and night.

And he shall be like a tree

planted by the rivers of water,

that bringeth forth his fruit in his season;

his leaf also shall not wither;

and whatsoever he doeth shall prosper.

The ungodly are not so:

but are like the chaff which the wind driveth away.

Therefore the ungodly shall not stand in the judgment,

nor sinners in the congregation of the righteous.

For the Lord knoweth the way of the righteous:

but the way of the ungodly shall perish.

Spring
By Lillian Cox

Drops of rain and bits of sunshine

Falling here and gleaming there,

Tiny blades of grass appearing.

Tell of springtime bright and fair.

Budding leaves are gently swaying,

Merry glad notes sweetly ring;

Robins, bluebirds, gaily singing,

Tell of happy, pleasant spring.

Violets, in blue and purple,

By the twinkling water clear;

Fair spring beauties, frail and dainty,

Tell the story, spring is here.

Cherry, peach, and apple blossoms

Scattering fragrance far and wide;

Buttercups and pure white snowdrops

Tell of gracious, sweet springtide.

Yielding to Temptation
From *The Burgess Animal Book for Children* by Thornton W. Burgess

"I know I ought to keep away from that garden," said Peter very meekly, "but you have no idea what a temptation it is. The things in that garden do taste so good."

Old Mother Nature turned her head to hide the twinkle in her eyes. When she turned toward Peter again her face was severe as before. "That is no excuse, Peter Rabbit," said she. "You should be sufficiently strong-minded not to yield to temptation. Yielding to temptation is the cause of most of the trouble in this world. It has made man an enemy to Jack Rabbit. Jack just cannot keep away from the crops planted by men. His family is very large, and when a lot of them get together in a field of clover or young wheat, or in a young orchard where the bark on the trees is tender and sweet, they do so much damage that the owner is hardly to be blamed for becoming angry and seeking to kill them. Yes, I am sorry to say, Jack Rabbit becomes a terrible nuisance when he goes where he has no business. Now I guess you have learned sufficient about your long-legged cousins. I've a great deal to do, so skip along home, both of you."

Exercise 134
The Squire
From *Treasure Island* by Robert Louis Stevenson

In the meantime, the squire and Captain Smollett were still on pretty distant terms with one another. The squire made no bones about the matter; he despised the captain. The captain, on his part, never spoke but when he was spoken to, and then sharp and short and dry, and not a word wasted. He owned, when driven into a corner, that he seemed to have been wrong about the crew, that some of them were as brisk as he wanted to see and all had behaved fairly well. As for the ship, he had taken a downright fancy to her. "She'll lie a point nearer the wind than a man has a right to expect of his own married wife, sir. But," he would add, "all I say is, we're not home again, and I don't like the cruise."

The squire, at this, would turn away and march up and down the deck, chin in the air.

"A trifle more of that man," he would say, "and I shall explode."

www.SimplyCharlotteMason.com   Spelling Wisdom, Book One, 151

Deer Mouse
From *The Burgess Animal Book for Children* by Thornton W. Burgess

When Peter and the others arrived for school the next morning, they found Whitefoot the Wood Mouse and Danny Meadow Mouse waiting with Old Mother Nature. Safe in her presence, they seemed to have lost much of their usual timidity. Whitefoot was sitting on the end of a log, and Danny was on the ground just beneath him.

"I want all the rest of you to look well at these two little cousins and notice how unlike two cousins can be," said Old Mother Nature. "Whitefoot, who is quite as often called Deer Mouse as Wood Mouse, is one of the prettiest of the entire Mouse family. I suspect he is called Deer Mouse because the upper part of his coat is such a beautiful fawn color. Notice that the upper side of his long slim tail is of the same color, while the under side is white, as is the whole under part of Whitefoot. Also those dainty feet are white, hence his name. See what big, soft black eyes he has, and notice that those delicate ears are of good size."

Except the Lord build the house,

they labor in vain that build it:

except the Lord keep the city,

the watchman waketh but in vain.

It is vain for you to rise up early,

to sit up late,

to eat the bread of sorrows:

for so he giveth his beloved sleep.

Lo, children are an heritage of the Lord:

and the fruit of the womb is his reward.

As arrows are in the hand of a mighty man;

so are children of the youth.

Happy is the man that hath his quiver full of them:

they shall not be ashamed,

but they shall speak with the enemies in the gate.

Plains

From *Home Geography for Primary Grades*

Let us imagine that we are out on a piece of nearly level land, many, many times larger than a playground. Such a broad, nearly level stretch of land is called a plain.

If this plain were covered with rich green grass and beautiful flowers, we should call it a prairie. In the summer it is a vast sea of waving grass. On the prairie we might find herds of wild horses and cattle, which feed upon the rich grass. If it were late in the summer, when the grass is dry and crisp, it might catch fire, and we might then see a grand sight: a prairie on fire.

We now come to another plain, miles and miles long, miles and miles wide. No rain falls here, and therefore we see no grass, nor flowers, nor cattle, nor horses, nothing but dry, burning sand, rocks, or gravel. We are in a desert. But we are so thirsty and tired!

No water to drink, no shade from the burning sun! Suddenly, in the midst of the desert, we come to a beautiful grassy spot. There is a cluster of date-palm trees, and, better still, a well or a spring of fresh water. This pleasant spot in the desert is called an oasis. Here we may quench our thirst and rest beneath the shade of the trees.

The Months
By Sara Coleridge

January brings the snow,
Makes our feet and fingers glow.

February brings the rain,
Thaws the frozen lake again.

March brings breezes loud and shrill,
Stirs the dancing daffodil.

April brings the primrose sweet,
Scatters daisies at their feet.

May brings flocks of pretty lambs,
Skipping by their fleecy dams.

June brings tulips, lilies, roses,
Fills the children's hands with posies.

Hot July brings cooling showers,
Apricots and gillyflowers.

August brings the sheaves of corn,
Then the harvest home is borne.

Warm September brings the fruit,
Sportsmen then begin to shoot.

Fresh October brings the pheasant,
Then to gather nuts is pleasant.

Dull November brings the blast,
Then the leaves are whirling fast.

Chill December brings the sleet,
Blazing fire and Christmas treat.

Whitefoot the Wood Mouse
From *The Burgess Animal Book for Children* by Thornton W. Burgess

So Whitefoot the Wood Mouse rarely ventures more than a few feet from a hiding place and safety. At the tiniest sound he starts nervously and often darts back into hiding without waiting to find out if there really is any danger. If he waited to make sure, he might wait too long, and it is better to be safe than sorry. If you and I had as many real frights in a year, not to mention false frights, as Whitefoot has in a day, we would, I suspect, lose our minds. Certainly we would be the most unhappy people in all the Great World.

But Whitefoot isn't unhappy. Not a bit of it. He is a very happy little fellow. There is a great deal of wisdom in that pretty little head of his. There is more real sense in it than in some very big heads. When some of his neighbors make fun of him for being so very, very timid, he doesn't try to pretend that he isn't afraid. He doesn't get angry. He simply says, "Of course I'm timid, very timid indeed. I'm afraid of almost everything. I would be foolish not to be. It is because I am afraid that I am alive and happy right now. I hope I shall never be less timid than I am now, for it would mean that sooner or later I would fail to run in time and would be gobbled up. It isn't cowardly to be timid when there is danger all around. Nor is it bravery to take a foolish and needless risk. So I seldom go far from home. It isn't safe for me, and I know it."

What the Winds Bring
By Lillian Cox

Comes the north wind, snowflakes bringing:

Robes the fields in purest white,

Paints grand houses, trees, and mountains

On our windowpanes at night.

Hills and vales the east wind visits,

Brings them chilly, driving rain;

Shivering cattle homeward hurry,

Onward through the darkening lane.

Heat the south wind kindly gives us;

Reddens apples, gilds the pear,

Gives the grape a richer purple,

Scatters plenty everywhere.

Flowers sweet the west wind offers,

Peeping forth from vines and trees;

Brings the butterflies so brilliant,

And the busy, humming bees.

Each wind brings his own best treasure

To our land from year to year;

Blessings many without measure

Ever attend the winds' career.

Bibliography
Spelling Wisdom, Book One

Adventures of Sherlock Holmes, The. Sir Arthur Conan Doyle.
Aesop's Fables.
Amusements in Mathematics. Henry Ernest Dudeney.
Andersen's Fairy Tales. Hans Christian Andersen.
"Ant, The." Oliver Herford.
"Arrow and the Song, The." Henry Wadsworth Longfellow.
"Bed in Summer." Robert Louis Stevenson.
Bible, The.
Black Beauty. Anna Sewell.
Burgess Animal Book for Children, The. Thornton W. Burgess
"Cradle Hymn." Martin Luther.
Deerslayer, The. James Fenimore Cooper.
Five Little Peppers and How They Grew. Margaret Sidney.
Friends and Helpers. Sarah J. Eddy.
Great Expectations. Charles Dickens.
"Happy Thought." Robert Louis Stevenson.
"He Prayeth Best." Samuel Taylor Coleridge.
Home Geography for Primary Grades
"Honor and Duty." Laura Ingalls Wilder.
"Lamb, The." William Blake.
The Letters of Wolfgang Amadeus Mozart. Wolfgang Amadeus Mozart.
Life of Jesus Christ for the Young, The. Richard Newton.
Little Women. Louisa May Alcott.
Long Voyage, The. Charles Dickens.
Merchant of Venice, The. William Shakespeare.
"Months, The." Sara Coleridge.
Mother West Wind "When" Stories. Thornton W. Burgess.
"My Heart Leaps Up When I Behold." William Wordsworth.
Oliver Twist. Charles Dickens.
"Owl, The." Alfred, Lord Tennyson.
Pioneers, The. James Fenimore Cooper.
"Pippa's Song." Robert Browning.
"Rain." Robert Louis Stevenson.
Robinson Crusoe. Daniel DeFoe.
Secret Garden, The. Frances Hodgson Burnett.
"Shepherd's Song, The." John Bunyan.
"Spring." Lillian Cox.
Swinton's Advanced Fourth Reader.
"Thought, A." Robert Louis Stevenson.

Treasure Box, The: A Third Reader. Mathilde C. Gecks, Charles E. Skinner, John W. Withers.

Treasure Island. Robert Louis Stevenson.

"Vowels: An Enigma, The." Jonathan Swift.

"What the Winds Bring." Lillian Cox.

"Whole Duty of Children." Robert Louis Stevenson.

Wind in the Willows, The. Kenneth Grahame.

Belongs, 122
Beloved, 153
Below, 131, 147
Ben, 104
Ben's, 110
Beneath, 100, 141, 142, 152, 154
Benjamin, 25, 34, 50, 61
Bent, 57, 107
Beside, 130
Besides, 137
Best, 27, 36, 54, 91, 114, 136, 157
Bet, 128
Better, 19, 61, 154, 156
Between, 113, 139, 140
Bewildered, 116
Bid, 102
Bien, 143
Big, 73, 97, 118, 152, 156
Bigger, 98
Bird, 53
Birds, 53, 126
Bit, 156
Bite, 105, 137
Bits, 149
Black, 93, 106, 137, 152
Bladder, 103
Blades, 145, 149
Blake, 102
Blamed, 150
Blast, 155
Blazing, 155
Bless, 102, 108
Blessed, 148
Blessings, 157
Blew, 121
Blight, 143
Bliss, 114
Bloom, 132, 133
Blossoms, 132, 149
Blowing, 55, 113
Blows, 62, 80, 101
Blue, 83, 95, 118, 126, 133, 146, 149
Bluebird, 129
Bluebirds, 149
Board, 113
Boast, 42
Boat, 83
Boats, 147
Boiled, 118
Boiling, 123
Boils, 144
Boll, 132
Bones, 151
Bonnets, 113
Book, 124, 140, 142, 150, 152, 156
Books, 27, 36, 55
Bore, 118
Bored, 142
Born, 135
Borne, 155
Both, 54, 98, 116, 150
Bother, 136

Bottle, 81
Bottom, 106, 109, 131
Bough, 117
Bought, 118
Bounced, 77
Bound, 90
Bowser, 124
Box, 78, 139
Boy, 123
Branch, 111, 117
Bravery, 156
Bread, 153
Break, 135
Breaking, 137
Breath, 117
Breathed, 120
Breathing, 104
Breeching, 137
Breezes, 155
Brick, 65
Bridle, 137
Bright, 102, 132, 138, 149
Brightness, 116
Brilliant, 157
Bring, 42, 127, 157
Bringeth, 148
Bringing, 157
Brings, 155, 157
Brisk, 151
Broad, 154
Brook, 80, 100, 106, 131, 147
Brother, 110, 113
Brothers, 60
Brought, 75
Brow, 98
Brown, 104, 118, 128
Brown's, 128
Brownie, 99
Browning, 84
Bubbles, 113
Bubbling, 147
Budding, 95, 149
Build, 135, 153
Builds, 53
Bunch, 111, 133
Bunyan, 114
Burden, 114
Burgess, 124, 129, 131, 142, 150, 152, 156
Burnett, 117
Burning, 86, 154
Burnished, 82
Burns, 144
Burst, 67
Bursts, 132
Bus, 77
Bush, 117
Business, 150
Bustle, 104
Busy, 80, 157
But, 46, 69, 72, 76, 83, 87, 89, 93, 94, 97, 98, 100, 103, 105, 107, 109, 110, 111, 116, 121, 122, 123, 124, 127, 128, 131, 136, 137, 138,

139, 140, 143, 144, 145, 148, 150, 151, 153, 154, 156
Butter, 118
Buttercups, 149
Butterflies, 119, 157
Butterfly, 119
Buy, 121
Buzz, 143
By, 18, 21, 23, 25, 27, 28, 29, 30, 32, 33, 34, 35, 36, 37, 40, 41, 43, 44, 48, 50, 52, 54, 55, 56, 57, 59, 61, 62, 64, 67, 69, 70, 71, 72, 73, 75, 76, 78, 79, 82, 83, 84, 85, 86, 87, 88, 90, 91, 92, 93, 97, 100, 101, 102, 104, 105, 106, 107, 109, 110, 111, 112, 113, 114, 115, 116, 117, 118, 119, 120, 121, 122, 123, 124, 125, 126, 127, 128, 129, 131, 132, 134, 136, 137, 138, 141, 142, 147, 148, 149, 150, 151, 152, 155, 156, 157

C

Cage, 82
Cake, 93
Calico, 132
Call, 94, 96, 145, 146, 154
Called, 94, 96, 102, 104, 125, 132, 133, 138, 139, 140, 146, 147, 152, 154
Calls, 102
Came, 96, 105, 111, 136
Camp, 91
Can, 18, 65, 68, 69, 78, 85, 88, 99, 101, 103, 106, 109, 120, 122, 123, 128, 138, 139, 140, 146, 147, 152
Candlelight, 126
Cannot, 21, 105, 109, 137, 144, 145, 150
Canoe, 69
Captain, 121, 151
Captain's, 121
Care, 71
Career, 157
Carefully, 53, 112
Carried, 147
Carry, 112, 137
Carrying, 100
Cart, 137
Cast, 91, 135
Cat, 97, 122
Catch, 88, 154
Catches, 25
Catching, 119
Cats, 122, 141
Cattle, 72, 154, 157
Caught, 88, 117, 124
Cause, 150
Caused, 119
Cell, 89, 103
Cells, 89
Center, 93
Certain, 87
Certainly, 92, 128, 142, 156

Chaff, 148
Chair, 76
Chaise, 137
Change, 121, 146
Changed, 144, 145
Changes, 145
Changing, 145
Charles, 27, 55, 62
Charlotte, 18
Chase, 134
Chat, 136
Cheap, 143
Checking, 127
Cheetah, 97
Cherry, 149
Chief, 139
Child, 41, 90, 102, 134, 137
Children, 35, 41, 110, 116, 124, 142, 150, 152, 153, 156
Children's, 155
Chill, 155
Chilly, 157
Chin, 151
Chirping, 136
Choose, 85, 143
Christ, 79, 109
Christian, 35, 59, 70, 86, 113, 116, 123, 127
Christmas, 155
Chuckled, 142
Churn, 47
City, 127, 153
Claws, 122
Clay, 113
Clean, 47, 82, 85
Clear, 59, 68, 87, 106, 126, 131, 138, 146, 149
Clever, 117
Click, 141
Close, 71, 89
Closed, 76
Cloth, 86, 127, 133
Clothes, 86, 121, 127
Clothing, 102, 133
Cloud, 146
Clouds, 146
Cloudy, 139
Clover, 150
Cluster, 154
Coal, 144
Coarse, 85
Coat, 121, 152
Cock, 141
Cocked, 67
Cocks, 121
Cold, 62, 96, 141, 145, 146
Coleridge, 54, 155
Collar, 137
Collected, 136
Color, 95, 146, 152
Colors, 146
Comb, 81
Come, 96, 101, 108, 115, 123, 129, 136, 141, 145, 154

Established, 46
Etc, 132
Evelyn, 98
Even, 64, 82, 83, 99, 103, 116, 137
Ever, 56, 65, 68, 114, 115, 121, 130, 132, 139, 157
Everlasting, 108
Every, 35, 61, 68, 135, 136, 137
Everybody, 82
Everyone, 86
Everything, 21, 60, 107, 110, 115, 123, 134, 156
Everywhere, 129, 157
Evil, 130
Exactly, 92, 109
Excellent, 49
Except, 104, 153
Excepting, 66
Excitement, 64
Excuse, 150
Exercise, 18, 19, 20, 21, 22, 23, 24, 25, 26, 27, 28, 29, 30, 31, 32, 33, 34, 35, 36, 37, 38, 39, 40, 41, 42, 43, 44, 45, 46, 47, 48, 49, 50, 51, 52, 53, 54, 55, 56, 57, 58, 59, 60, 61, 62, 63, 64, 65, 66, 67, 68, 69, 70, 71, 72, 73, 74, 75, 76, 77, 78, 79, 80, 81, 82, 83, 84, 85, 86, 87, 88, 89, 90, 91, 92, 93, 94, 95, 96, 97, 98, 99, 100, 101, 102, 103, 104, 105, 106, 107, 108, 109, 110, 111, 112, 113, 114, 115, 116, 117, 118, 119, 120, 121, 122, 123, 124, 125, 126, 127, 128, 129, 130, 131, 132, 133, 134, 135, 136, 137, 138, 139, 140, 141, 142, 143, 144, 145, 146, 147, 148, 149, 150, 151, 152, 153, 154, 155, 156, 157
Exertions, 115
Exhausted, 48
Expect, 101, 151
Expectations, 62
Explain, 143
Explode, 151
Eyes, 73, 76, 124, 150, 152

F

Face, 115, 118, 125, 150
Fail, 64, 128, 156
Failed, 128
Fair, 51, 60, 149
Fairly, 151
Fairy, 123
Faithful, 101
Fall, 114, 146
Fallen, 81, 121
Falling, 146, 147, 149
Falls, 29, 146, 147, 154
False, 156
Family, 53, 70, 118, 122, 150, 152
Fancy, 151
Far, 27, 41, 97, 129, 140, 149, 156
Farmer, 118

Far-off, 141
Farthest, 138
Fast, 73, 96, 113, 137, 155
Fatal, 112
Father, 60, 90
Father-care, 60
Fawn, 152
Fear, 114, 124, 130
Feasible, 91
Feather-clouds, 146
Feathers, 119
Features, 78
February, 66, 155
Feed, 102, 154
Feelings, 93
Feet, 122, 126, 133, 140, 152, 155, 156
Fell, 100, 120
Fellow, 156
Fenimore, 40, 57, 64, 69, 71
Few, 111, 156
Fibers, 133
Fido, 134
Field, 29, 106, 132, 133, 136, 150
Fields, 53, 96, 157
Fierce, 122
Fifteen, 87
Fifth, 78
Filled, 59
Fills, 155
Finally, 115
Find, 45, 53, 61, 78, 109, 123, 125, 138, 139, 140, 154, 156
Finds, 147
Fine, 85, 88, 101
Fingers, 155
Finish, 86
Finished, 107
Fir, 106, 116
Fire, 55, 144, 154, 155
First, 21, 24, 52, 73, 74, 101, 103, 106, 129, 132, 138
Fish, 88, 131
Fisher, 88
Fishing, 88
Five, 93, 104, 110, 115, 141
Fixed, 137
Flakes, 146
Flat, 142
Flavor, 43
Flax, 133
Fleecy, 146, 155
Flew, 96, 120
Flight, 120
Float, 147
Floating, 144, 146
Floats, 145
Flock, 104
Flocks, 155
Floor, 77, 81
Flowers, 95, 132, 133, 154, 157
Flows, 147
Flu, 94
Flutter, 113, 119

Fluttering, 96
Fly, 78, 115
Fog, 146
Folding-doors, 116
Folks, 28, 59
Follow, 120, 130
Followed, 116, 124
Follows, 124
Food, 60, 136
Fool, 124
Foolish, 156
Foot, 91, 140
For, 18, 32, 42, 46, 50, 54, 58, 60, 64, 70, 72, 79, 81, 83, 85, 88, 91, 99, 102, 104, 105, 108, 109, 110, 113, 116, 118, 120, 121, 123, 124, 125, 127, 128, 129, 130, 132, 133, 136, 137, 138, 139, 140, 142, 143, 144, 145, 146, 147, 148, 150, 151, 152, 153, 154, 156
Forehead, 123
Forelock, 101
Forest, 71, 99
Forever, 46, 142
Forfeit, 128
Fork, 107, 117
Forlorn, 93, 115
Form, 79, 95, 132, 146, 147
Formed, 93
Forms, 146
Forth, 42, 121, 148, 157
Fortune, 59
Forwards, 113
Found, 87, 101, 120, 124, 136, 152
Fountain, 80
Four, 73, 118
Fourth, 78, 80, 89, 95, 103
Fox, 25, 111, 124
Fragrance, 149
Frail, 149
Frances, 117
Franklin, 25, 34, 50, 61
Freedom, 91
Freeze, 146
Freezes, 146
Frequently, 112
Fresh, 154, 155
Friday, 47
Friend, 92, 120
Friends, 60, 85, 112, 119, 122
Frights, 156
Frocks, 113
From, 27, 40, 44, 55, 57, 59, 62, 64, 67, 69, 70, 71, 72, 75, 76, 78, 79, 80, 82, 83, 85, 86, 87, 89, 91, 92, 93, 94, 95, 97, 101, 103, 104, 105, 106, 107, 109, 110, 112, 113, 114, 115, 116, 117, 118, 119, 120, 121, 122, 123, 124, 125, 127, 128, 129, 131, 132, 133, 134, 135, 136, 137, 138, 139, 140, 142, 143, 144, 145, 146, 147, 150, 151, 152, 154, 156, 157

Frozen, 155
Fruit, 148, 153, 155
Full, 23, 35, 95, 153
Full-grown, 103
Fullness, 114
Fully, 83
Fun, 143, 156
Funny, 129, 131, 142
Fur, 73
Further, 143
Future, 110, 112

G

Gaily, 149
Gaily-dressed, 59
Galley, 82
Gallivant, 134
Garden, 117, 118, 150
Gardens, 95
Gas, 144
Gate, 106, 153
Gates, 108
Gather, 135, 146, 155
Gaunt, 143
Gave, 101, 102
Gaze, 95
Gazing, 131
Generations, 108
Gentle, 122
Gently, 149
Geography, 125, 132, 133, 138, 139, 140, 144, 145, 146, 147, 154
Get, 40, 69, 92, 99, 109, 126, 135, 143, 144, 150, 156
Gets, 144
Getting, 105, 127
Gilds, 157
Gillyflowers, 155
Gin, 132
Girl, 118
Girls, 113
Give, 105, 111, 128
Given, 45, 75, 93, 138
Gives, 43, 66, 157
Giveth, 153
Giving, 75
Glad, 82, 129, 143, 149
Gladness, 108
Glanced, 76
Glare, 116
Glass, 78
Gleaming, 149
Glory, 63
Glow, 155
Go, 60, 85, 88, 94, 97, 99, 101, 114, 126, 132, 137, 144, 147, 15
Gobbled, 156
God, 54, 74, 102, 108, 114
God's, 84
Goes, 141, 150
Going, 124, 126, 139
Gold, 51, 96
Gone, 87, 96

Good, 70, 91, 108, 123, 143, 150, 152
Goodness, 60, 130
Got, 100, 101, 107, 115, 143
Grace, 35
Graceful, 122
Gracious, 149
Grades, 125, 132, 133, 138, 139, 140, 144, 145, 146, 147, 154
Grahame, 83, 107
Grain, 136
Grand, 154, 157
Grape, 157
Grapes, 111
Grass, 107, 124, 145, 149, 154
Grasshopper, 136
Grassy, 154
Gravel, 154
Great, 33, 39, 54, 62, 110, 121, 132, 136, 137, 138, 150, 156
Greater, 74, 111
Greatly, 109
Green, 70, 95, 113, 117, 130, 132, 154
Grew, 73, 93, 104, 106, 110, 115
Grieves, 143
Grocerman, 118
Ground, 141, 142, 147, 152
Group, 138
Grove, 106
Grow, 63, 88, 89, 90, 96, 103, 119, 133
Growing, 131
Grown-up, 126
Grows, 103, 133
Grudge, 105
Guess, 124, 150
Guidance, 60
Guide, 114, 139

H

Had, 59, 71, 73, 76, 81, 82, 83, 86, 87, 91, 93, 96, 99, 100, 104, 105, 107, 111, 117, 121, 127, 131, 136, 142, 151, 156
Hail, 146
Half, 76, 92, 117
Halfway, 139
Hand, 85, 113, 125, 153
Handle, 138
Hands, 101, 119, 143, 155
Hang, 121
Hanging, 82, 91, 113, 145
Hans, 59, 70, 86, 113, 116, 123, 127
Happened, 88, 100, 112
Happens, 144, 145
Happiness, 28, 93
Happy, 23, 28, 70, 129, 149, 153, 56
Hard, 109, 115, 126, 129, 134
Hardly, 109, 150
Harmless, 119
Harness, 137

Harvest, 155
Has, 66, 79, 85, 94, 103, 113, 120, 124, 134, 137, 150, 151, 152, 156
Hasn't, 124
Haste, 38
Hasty, 87, 119
Hat, 118, 121
Hate, 135
Hath, 49, 66, 108, 141, 153
Hauled, 83
Have, 30, 32, 39, 44, 55, 66, 67, 88, 93, 94, 100, 101, 104, 107, 112, 114, 119, 122, 125, 126, 136, 137, 138, 139, 140, 143, 145, 146, 150, 151, 152
Having, 75, 121
Hawker, 121
Hay, 72, 141
He, 41, 49, 54, 67, 72, 76, 79, 82, 83, 91, 97, 98, 99, 100, 102, 107, 108, 111, 112, 113, 114, 116, 117, 118, 121, 124, 127, 129, 130, 131, 136, 137, 139, 142, 143, 148, 150, 151, 152, 153, 156
Head, 57, 67, 70, 72, 76, 130, 131, 150, 156
Heads, 73, 96, 156
Heal, 135
Health, 60
Healthy, 34
Hear, 126
Heard, 96, 127, 140
Hears, 129
Heart, 74, 83, 90, 120
Heart's, 136
Heat, 157
Heating, 145
Heaven, 60, 84, 135
Hedge, 106
Heels, 129
Hehe, 143
Held, 119
Hello, 142
Help, 110
Helpers, 85, 112, 119, 122
Helping, 136
Hence, 152
Henry, 87, 92, 120
Her, 81, 85, 94, 98, 110, 115, 117, 118, 122, 134, 150, 151, 152
Herald, 129
Herds, 154
Here, 29, 60, 114, 123, 142, 149, 154
Hereafter, 88, 114
Herford, 134
Heritage, 153
Hesitate, 91
Hide, 150
Hiding, 124, 156
High, 131, 133, 146, 147
Hills, 157
Hillside's, 84
Him, 64, 82, 99, 107, 108, 124,

127, 129, 131, 137, 142, 152, 156
Himself, 102, 113, 121, 127, 142
Hint, 143
Hire, 22
His, 22, 33, 49, 57, 60, 63, 67, 72, 76, 77, 79, 82, 84, 99, 100, 102, 108, 111, 112, 113, 114, 116, 117, 118, 121, 123, 124, 127, 129, 130, 131, 134, 137, 141, 142, 148, 150, 151, 152, 153, 156, 157
Hodgson, 117
Hoe, 117
Hold, 113
Holds, 40, 70, 144
Hole, 77, 112
Holiday, 59, 93, 104
Hollow, 73, 103
Holmes, 67, 76, 97
Home, 53, 56, 60, 73, 99, 100, 115, 118, 125, 132, 133, 134, 138, 139, 140, 141, 144, 145, 146, 147, 150, 151, 154, 155, 156
Homes, 53
Homesick, 115
Homeward, 157
Honor, 128
Hope, 68, 91, 105, 143, 156
Hopes, 93
Hopping, 126, 136
Horribly, 91
Horse, 58, 137
Horses, 137, 138, 154
Hospital, 94
Hot, 62, 111, 119, 144, 155
Hound, 124
Hour, 87, 104, 117
House, 104, 106, 119, 122, 130, 140, 153
Houses, 65, 157
How, 63, 65, 86, 93, 103, 104, 110, 115, 117, 127, 128, 134, 138, 139, 140, 146, 152
Howard, 56
However, 119, 127
Humble, 56, 114
Humming, 157
Humor, 91
Hundred, 85
Hunger, 136
Hungry, 137
Hunts, 124
Hurries, 134
Hurry, 157
Hut, 57
Hutter, 69
Hymn, 72

I

I, 18, 32, 37, 48, 55, 63, 68, 72, 75, 88, 90, 91, 92, 94, 97, 98, 101, 102, 103, 106, 111, 114, 120, 121, 123, 124, 126, 127, 128, 130, 136, 137, 142, 143, 150, 151, 152, 156

I'll, 102, 128
I'm, 23, 98, 156
I've, 124, 150
Ice, 146
Idea, 150
If, 24, 53, 70, 75, 78, 81, 88, 92, 93, 101, 109, 116, 119, 142, 144, 145, 146, 154, 156
Ignorant, 127
Imaginations, 115
Imagine, 154
Immensely, 70
In, 21, 33, 35, 38, 51, 53, 55, 60, 62, 63, 68, 69, 70, 71, 72, 73, 76, 77, 78, 80, 81, 82, 83, 84, 85, 86, 87, 89, 90, 91, 92, 93, 95, 96, 97, 98, 100, 103, 104, 105, 106, 107, 109, 110, 111, 112, 113, 116, 117, 118, 119, 120, 121, 122, 123, 125, 126, 127, 128, 129, 130, 131, 132, 133, 134, 136, 137, 138, 139, 141, 143, 144, 145, 146, 147, 148, 149, 150, 151, 152, 153, 154, 156, 157
Inch, 140
Inches, 140
Increased, 115
Indeed, 131, 143, 156
Indian, 57
Industrious, 85
Inferior, 27
Inform, 94, 143
Ingalls, 128
Instead, 136
Intelligence, 112, 127
Intense, 71
Into, 69, 77, 80, 81, 83, 88, 100, 105, 106, 108, 120, 123, 131, 132, 133, 144, 145, 146, 147, 151, 156
Iron, 47
Is, 22, 23, 26, 29, 33, 35, 37, 40, 41, 43, 46, 48, 49, 50, 51, 55, 62, 70, 72, 74, 78, 79, 80, 85, 87, 90, 92, 94, 96, 97, 98, 99, 101, 102, 103, 107, 108, 109, 112, 113, 114, 119, 122, 124, 125, 126, 129, 130, 132, 133, 135, 136, 137, 138, 139, 140, 141, 142, 144, 145, 146, 147, 148, 149, 150, 151, 152, 153, 154, 155, 156
Island, 82, 91, 101, 121, 151
Isn't, 124, 142, 156
It, 29, 30, 33, 35, 43, 45, 56, 59, 62, 66, 67, 70, 73, 77, 78, 79, 80, 83, 87, 88, 90, 91, 93, 97, 99, 100, 101, 103, 104, 105, 106, 107, 108, 109, 112, 113, 114, 115, 116, 117, 118, 120, 121, 124, 125, 126, 128, 129, 131, 132, 134, 136, 137, 138, 139, 140, 142, 143, 144, 145, 146, 147, 150, 153, 154, 156
It's, 101
Its, 43, 60, 83, 89, 97, 104, 105, 120, 132, 136, 138, 140, 147
Itself, 80, 136

Mighty, 153
Mild, 102
Mile, 140
Miles, 31, 87, 154
Milk, 97, 118
Milkmaids, 141
Milliliter, 98
Million, 119
Mills, 132
Mind, 74, 75, 79, 100, 132
Minds, 28, 79, 156
Mine, 130
Miner, 142
Mingled, 132
Minute, 146
Minute's, 115
Missed, 111
Mist, 146
Mister, 67
Mistress, 129
Moiling, 136
Moist, 117
Moisture, 146
Mole, 83, 107, 142
Mole's, 83
Mom, 81, 94
Moment, 46, 116, 123
Monday, 47
Money, 30, 128
Months, 155
Moon, 143
More, 66, 69, 80, 85, 87, 100, 123, 124, 129, 151, 156
Moreover, 85
Morn, 84, 134
Morning, 60, 72, 84, 118, 145, 152
Morning's, 84
Morrow, 93
Morsel, 111
Most, 28, 85, 121, 122, 124, 150, 156
Mother, 73, 81, 93, 104, 110, 118, 123, 129, 131, 150, 152
Mother's, 115
Mother-love, 60
Motor, 77, 87
Motto, 18
Mountain, 147
Mountains, 147, 157
Mountainside, 147
Mourn, 135
Mouse, 124, 152, 156
Mouth, 100
Move, 124
Mozart, 143
Mr., 101, 128
Much, 88, 93, 107, 109, 114, 119, 124, 126, 128, 140, 142, 143, 150, 152
Muscles, 94
Muslin, 132
Must, 37, 101, 115, 125, 137, 140, 143, 144, 147

Mustard, 107
Muttering, 105
My, 67, 72, 75, 88, 90, 91, 93, 111, 123, 124, 127, 128, 130, 134, 142, 143
Myself, 75, 124

N

Nail, 58, 81
Name, 102, 108, 138, 152
Name's, 130
Named, 118
Namely, 74
Names, 68, 125
Nap, 105
Natural, 90
Nature, 150, 152
Nay, 88
Near, 105, 142, 146
Nearer, 151
Nearly, 154
Necessary, 109
Necessity, 136
Need, 99
Needle, 139
Needles, 86
Needless, 156
Needs, 94, 114
Neighbor, 74
Neighbors, 61, 121, 127, 156
Neither, 137, 139
Nervously, 156
Nest, 73, 136
Never, 30, 48, 78, 100, 107, 121, 124, 134, 137, 151, 156
New, 60, 61, 82, 86, 124, 127
New-mown, 141
Newton, 79, 109
Next, 118, 152
Nice, 35, 118
Nigh, 72
Night, 60, 68, 72, 86, 115, 126, 134, 138, 139, 143, 148, 157
No, 25, 56, 69, 71, 72, 73, 91, 97, 99, 111, 114, 115, 121, 130, 134, 136, 142, 150, 151, 154
Noise, 71, 108
None, 74, 121, 129
Noon, 59, 92
Nooo, 128
Nor, 137, 139, 148, 154, 156
North, 125, 138, 139, 157
Northeast, 139
Northwest, 139
Nose, 111, 118, 124
Not, 32, 37, 42, 48, 50, 63, 71, 83, 87, 88, 91, 95, 97, 98, 99, 103, 107, 108, 115, 116, 119, 120, 122, 126, 128, 129, 130, 133, 136, 137, 138, 140, 144, 148, 150, 151, 153, 156
Note, 94
Notes, 149

Nothing, 39, 83, 121, 123, 127, 154
Notice, 65, 152
Noticed, 115, 146
Nov., 143
November, 66, 155
Now, 67, 75, 76, 88, 90, 91, 92, 100, 101, 104, 116, 123, 128, 132, 142, 143, 145, 147, 150, 154, 156
Nowhere, 129
Nuisance, 150
Number, 23
Nutmeg, 118
Nuts, 155

O

Oak, 89, 120
Oasis, 154
Obeyed, 82
Object, 140
Objects, 140
Observe, 103, 134
Observed, 83
Observing, 48
Occasion, 93
Ocean, 109, 147
October, 118, 155
Odors, 95
Of, 22, 23, 27, 31, 35, 36, 41, 42, 43, 44, 46, 49, 50, 51, 53, 55, 58, 59, 60, 62, 63, 64, 65, 67, 68, 69, 71, 75, 76, 77, 78, 79, 80, 81, 82, 85, 86, 87, 89, 90, 92, 93, 95, 96, 97, 98, 99, 100, 102, 103, 104, 105, 106, 107, 108, 109, 110, 111, 112, 115, 116, 117, 118, 119, 120, 121, 122, 123, 124, 127, 128, 129, 130, 131, 132, 133, 135, 136, 137, 138, 139, 140, 142, 143, 144, 145, 146, 147, 148, 149, 150, 151, 152, 153, 154, 155, 156
Off, 77, 86, 88, 112, 116, 119, 147
Offend, 39
Offers, 157
Office, 127
Often, 105, 138, 140, 145, 152, 156
Oh, 52, 93
Oil, 130
Old, 90, 104, 112, 122, 123, 150, 152
Older, 110, 113, 116
Oldest, 104
Oliver, 27, 134
On, 19, 20, 21, 24, 25, 26, 28, 29, 30, 31, 36, 38, 47, 48, 50, 52, 58, 72, 77, 79, 80, 81, 83, 84, 86, 91, 93, 94, 96, 97, 100, 101, 104, 106, 107, 111, 113, 114, 119, 121, 124, 126, 127, 128, 131, 133, 136, 137, 138, 139, 142, 144, 145, 146, 147, 150, 151, 152, 154, 157
Once, 83, 99, 101, 118, 137, 138
One, 21, 31, 57, 62, 63, 66, 70,

77, 78, 79, 81, 82, 85, 89, 92, 96, 99, 103, 106, 110, 111, 112, 113, 115, 116, 118, 121, 122, 123, 124, 127, 131, 136, 137, 139, 142, 151, 152
Ones, 116
Only, 66, 88, 99, 110, 116, 121, 122, 142
Onward, 157
Onwards, 77
Open, 77, 81, 95, 121, 131, 132
Opened, 45, 73, 76, 100, 116
Opinion, 79
Opposite, 125
Or, 53, 55, 65, 71, 79, 80, 85, 87, 90, 98, 101, 103, 114, 117, 121, 124, 126, 127, 132, 133, 137, 139, 140, 141, 146, 147, 150, 154, 156
Orange, 95
Orchard, 111, 150
Order, 125
Ordinarily, 109
Organ, 64
Other, 57, 65, 74, 78, 79, 92, 99, 106, 109, 110, 113, 116, 126, 137, 138, 139, 147
Others, 65, 105, 109, 112, 138, 152
Ought, 18, 107, 123, 150
Our, 79, 87, 91, 92, 95, 106, 122, 154, 155, 156, 157
Ourselves, 108
Out, 53, 75, 77, 81, 83, 100, 105, 107, 117, 122, 138, 140, 142, 143, 147, 154, 156
Outside, 83
Over, 70, 75, 80, 87, 93, 96, 102, 103, 106, 111, 115, 119, 130, 142
Overhung, 106
Overwhelmingly, 110
Owing, 87
Owl, 141
Own, 89, 100, 127, 137, 151, 157
Owned, 151
Owner, 150
Ox, 105

P

Paces, 111
Packed, 89, 107
Packing, 107
Padded, 122
Paddle, 69
Painted, 83
Paints, 157
Palaces, 56
Pale, 132
Panted, 98
Papa, 143
Parents, 81
Parks, 53
Parrot, 82
Part, 91, 121, 138, 151, 152
Particles, 146

Particular, 82, 85
Parts, 27
Party, 57
Pass, 65, 144
Passed, 136
Past, 126
Pasture, 108
Pastures, 130
Patched, 121
Patches, 121
Paths, 130
Patient, 85
Paused, 98
Paws, 112
Payne, 56
Peace, 39, 61, 100, 135
Peach, 149
Pear, 157
Pearls, 145
Pebbles, 131
Peeked, 81
Peeping, 157
Pence, 143
Penny, 26
People, 37, 65, 99, 105, 108, 119, 127, 138, 156
People's, 126
Peppers, 93, 104, 110, 115
Perceive, 143
Perfectly, 142
Perhaps, 65
Perish, 148
Perseverance, 24
Person, 79, 127
Persons, 116
Peter, 124, 129, 131, 142, 150, 152
Pheasant, 155
Picked, 81, 118, 132
Picture, 132
Piece, 100, 154
Piety, 90
Pilgrimage, 114
Pin, 82, 103, 139
Pint, 118
Pioneers, 57, 64
Pipe, 113
Pippa's, 84
Pirates, 91
Place, 35, 56, 69, 86, 106, 116, 125, 131, 140, 156
Places, 109
Plain, 154
Plains, 154
Plank, 100
Plans, 110
Plant, 89, 132, 133, 135
Planted, 118, 135, 148, 150
Plants, 95, 103, 131
Plate, 107
Play, 96, 126, 134
Playground, 154
Pleasant, 106, 107, 115, 149, 154, 155

Please, 94
Pleasures, 56
Plenty, 136, 157
Plow, 138
Plowed, 106
Pluck, 135
Pod, 132, 133
Point, 101, 103, 138, 143, 151
Pointed, 107
Pointing, 125
Points, 139
Polish, 81
Polly, 115
Polly's, 110
Pond, 80, 106
Pool, 131
Poor, 115
Popped, 77
Portrait, 143
Posies, 155
Possess, 127
Pot, 107, 118
Poultry, 25
Poured, 123
Powerful, 64, 122
Practice, 20, 52
Prairie, 154
Praise, 108
Pray, 76, 88
Prayeth, 54
Preach, 20
Precious, 143
Precise, 76
Prefer, 91, 127
Prejudice, 79
Prelate's, 143
Prepare, 136
Preparest, 130
Presence, 108, 130, 152
Present, 116, 136
Presented, 93, 104
Pressed, 132
Pretend, 143, 156
Pretended, 86
Prettiest, 152
Pretty, 87, 89, 119, 132, 133, 151, 155, 156
Prevailed, 71
Pride, 114
Primary, 125, 132, 133, 138, 139, 140, 144, 145, 146, 147, 154
Primrose, 155
Principal, 104
Probably, 112
Procession, 86
Professor, 92
Promise, 143
Promptly, 112
Proper, 104, 138
Property, 127
Propose, 101
Prosper, 148
Proudly, 98
Prove, 91, 127

Proverb, 19, 20, 24, 26, 31, 38, 58
Proverbs, 42, 46, 49, 51
Provoked, 67
Psalm, 39, 108, 130, 148, 153
Pulled, 116
Pure, 124, 129, 149
Purest, 95, 157
Purple, 95, 149, 157
Purpose, 135
Pursue, 78
Pushed, 142
Pushing, 112
Pussy, 122
Put, 88, 96, 118, 123, 128, 137, 144

Q

Quart, 98
Quarter, 92
Queen, 113
Queer, 131, 142
Quench, 111, 154
Question, 67, 87
Quick, 124
Quickly, 145
Quiet, 104, 131
Quieted, 104
Quietly, 116, 137
Quite, 93, 107, 116, 122, 126, 131, 138, 142, 143, 152
Quiver, 153

R

Rabbit, 129, 131, 150
Racing, 115
Rackbrane, 92
Rage, 105
Rain, 29, 55, 59, 146, 147, 149, 154, 155, 157
Rainbow, 90
Raining, 29
Rains, 29
Rainy, 70
Rake, 40
Ralph, 32, 33, 36, 37
Rare, 94
Rarely, 141, 156
Rat, 83, 107, 112
Rate, 69, 87
Rather, 127
Rats, 112
Razor, 81
Reach, 109
Reached, 109
Read, 55
Reader, 80, 89, 95, 103
Ready, 86, 115, 132
Real, 131, 156
Really, 70, 156
Received, 121, 143
Receiving, 112
Recent, 87
Reckless, 112
Recommend, 136

Red, 95, 96
Reddens, 157
Reddy, 124
Reddy's, 124
Redoubled, 115
Re-echoed, 116
Reflected, 100
Reflection, 100
Refrain, 135
Rejoice, 102
Rejoices, 129
Rejoicing, 116
Released, 119
Relish, 75
Remain, 144
Remarkable, 112
Remember, 106, 121
Remembered, 127
Remind, 95
Rend, 135
Repent, 38
Replied, 98, 128
Rescue, 112
Respected, 82
Rest, 47, 60, 66, 118, 124, 129, 139, 152, 154
Restoreth, 130
Return, 87
Returning, 105
Reward, 153
Rhymes, 143
Ribbons, 113
Rich, 154
Richard, 64, 79, 109
Richer, 157
Rid, 144
Ride, 77, 87
Rider, 58
Ridge, 142
Ridges, 142
Right, 84, 94, 123, 125, 131, 142, 151, 156
Righteous, 148
Righteousness, 130
Rill, 147
Rills, 147
Ring, 149
Ripe, 118
Ripening, 111
Ripens, 132
Ripples, 80
Rise, 34, 93, 101, 125, 142, 153
Rises, 145, 146, 147
Risk, 127, 128, 156
River, 88, 147
Rivers, 148
Roads, 87
Roadside, 106
Roam, 56
Roared, 77
Robert, 23, 29, 35, 41, 82, 84, 9
101, 121, 126, 151
Robes, 157
Robins, 149

Robinson, 75
Rocks, 154
Rod, 130
Rogues, 86
Roll, 86
Roof, 80, 142
Room, 104, 121, 140, 144
Roots, 117
Rope, 83
Roses, 155
Round, 103, 111, 113, 116, 118, 134, 141
Roundelay, 141
Route, 87
Row, 119
Rubbed, 119
Rug, 77
Ruler, 140
Rum, 121
Run, 111, 141, 156
Runneth, 130
Running, 100, 106
Runs, 147
Rush, 112
Rushed, 116
Rushes, 80, 106

S

Sac, 103
Sad, 129
Saddle, 137
Safe, 19, 143, 152, 156
Safely, 143
Safety, 19, 156
Said, 67, 69, 76, 83, 88, 96, 111, 123, 127, 136, 142, 150, 152
Sail, 141
Sailing, 109
Sailor, 139
Sailors, 138
Sake, 130
Salesman, 67
Salt, 118
Same, 87, 89, 109, 118, 122, 136, 152
Samuel, 48, 54
Sand, 154
Sands, 143
Sank, 146
Sara, 155
Sarah, 85, 112, 119, 122
Sat, 86, 131
Satin, 73
Satisfying, 97
Saturday, 47
Saucer, 97
Saved, 26
Savest, 114
Saving, 26
Saw, 48, 99, 100, 107, 112, 136, 42
Say, 41, 63, 75, 92, 93, 119, 123, 34, 138, 143, 150, 151

Saying, 35, 101, 111
Says, 123, 156
Scattering, 149
Scatters, 155, 157
Scent, 124
Scheme, 91
School, 152
Scissors, 86
Score, 66
Scornful, 148
Scott, 52
Scratch, 40
Screen, 71
Sea, 29, 75, 138, 145, 154
Seachest, 121
Searching, 81
Season, 135, 148
Seat, 148
Second, 74, 101
Secret, 110, 117
Security, 128
See, 48, 68, 75, 78, 81, 82, 86, 103, 126, 127, 131, 132, 137, 144, 145, 146, 151, 152, 154
Seed, 89, 103, 118, 132
Seeing, 125
Seek, 45, 57
Seeking, 150
Seem, 99, 126, 131, 146
Seemed, 131, 151, 152
Seeming, 129
Seems, 119, 125
Seen, 32, 95, 100, 107, 121, 139, 145, 146
Sees, 137
Seized, 112
Seizes, 134
Seizure, 143
Seldom, 64, 156
Sell, 143
Send, 143
Sending, 127
Sends, 60
Sense, 143, 156
Sent, 132
Separate, 85, 132
Separated, 57
September, 66, 155
Serenity, 33
Serpent, 44
Serve, 108
Served, 71
Service, 82
Set, 78, 99, 112, 119, 125
Setter, 143
Seven, 84, 138
Severe, 150
Sew, 135
Sewed, 86
Sewell, 106, 137
Shade, 62, 117, 154
Shadow, 100, 130
Shady, 106
Shakes, 80

Shakespeare, 44
Shall, 39, 45, 46, 69, 88, 90, 95, 109, 114, 130, 143, 148, 151, 153, 156
Shalt, 74
Shape, 146
Sharp, 122, 151
Shave, 81
She, 85, 94, 98, 115, 117, 118, 122, 129, 134, 150
She'll, 151
Sheaves, 155
Sheep, 108
Shelter, 60
Shepherd, 130
Shepherd's, 114
Sherlock, 67, 76, 97
Shines, 62
Shingles, 119
Ship, 75, 151
Ships, 29
Shivering, 157
Shivery, 129
Shoe, 58, 143
Shoes, 59
Shoot, 155
Shop, 118
Short, 140, 142, 151
Shot, 120
Should, 23, 41, 78, 91, 104, 116, 126, 127, 131, 146, 150, 154
Shouted, 116
Show, 124
Showed, 117
Showers, 155
Shown, 112
Shows, 139
Shrill, 155
Shut, 73
Side, 91, 106, 152
Sides, 147
Sidney, 93, 104, 110, 115
Sight, 117, 120, 122, 132, 133, 134, 142, 154
Silence, 135
Silk, 113
Silver, 91
Silver's, 91
Simple, 87
Simpleton, 127
Simply, 142, 156
Singing, 96, 108, 136, 149
Sinks, 147
Sinners, 148
Sir, 52, 67, 76, 97, 101, 151
Sister, 110
Sisters, 60
Sit, 55, 153
Sits, 141
Sitteth, 148
Sitting, 107, 113, 152
Six, 85
Sixteen, 86
Size, 83, 152

Sketched, 91
Skin, 133
Skip, 150
Skipping, 155
Sky, 68, 72, 90, 126, 138, 146
Sleep, 153
Sleeping, 25
Sleeps, 134
Sleet, 55, 155
Slender, 85
Slim, 152
Slope, 147
Sloth, 25
Slow, 137
Slumber, 105
Small, 54, 65, 88, 97, 122, 133, 146, 147
Smart, 124
Smells, 141
Smiling, 131
Smoke, 144
Smollett, 101, 151
Smooth, 73
Snail's, 84
Snap, 100
Snout, 51
Snow, 96, 113, 146, 155
Snowdrops, 149
Snowflakes, 157
Snowy, 132
Snub, 118
So, 23, 51, 56, 70, 71, 86, 90, 93, 98, 100, 109, 110, 116, 120, 126, 129, 137, 138, 142, 147, 148, 150, 153, 154, 156, 157
Soap, 113
Sock, 81
Soft, 73, 96, 119, 122, 129, 152
Softest, 102
Softly, 122
Soil, 142
Solomon, 63
Some, 65, 68, 82, 101, 104, 105, 106, 109, 110, 118, 119, 121, 123, 124, 127, 128, 138, 140, 145, 147, 151, 156
Somebody, 127
Somehow, 107, 131
Something, 48, 79, 116, 142
Sometimes, 124, 129, 146
Somewhere, 144
Song, 84, 114, 120, 143
Songs, 96
Soon, 73, 88, 95, 96, 105, 119, 123, 143
Sooner, 101, 156
Sorrows, 153
Sorry, 19, 150, 156
Sort, 103, 123
Soul, 74, 130
Souls, 110
Sound, 156
Sounds, 129
Sour, 111

South, 125, 138, 139, 157
Southeast, 139
Southwest, 139
Spade, 117
Spangled, 85
Spareth, 49
Speak, 41, 135, 137, 153
Speech, 64
Speed, 87
Spell, 104
Spend, 30
Spice, 43
Spider, 85
Spin, 63, 85
Spirit, 49
Spit, 77
Splendid, 116
Splendor, 116
Spoke, 92, 121, 151
Spoken, 41, 151
Sponge, 144
Spoon, 143
Spoons, 118
Sport, 119
Sportsmen, 155
Spot, 154
Spouts, 80
Spring, 84, 112, 129, 147, 149, 154
Springtide, 149
Springtime, 95, 149
Sprouted, 118
Spun, 132, 133
Spy, 75
Squander, 50
Squash, 118
Squashes, 118
Squeak, 124
Squealed, 77
Squeezed, 115
Squire, 151
Squirrel, 73
Squirrels, 73
Staff, 130
Stairs, 112
Stalk, 133
Stand, 137, 148
Standeth, 148
Stands, 113
Star, 138
Staring, 107
Stars, 68, 72, 138, 139
Start, 137
Starting, 31
Starts, 103, 156
State, 116
Stay, 72
Steep, 106, 131
Step, 31, 112, 147
Stepped, 83
Stevenson, 23, 29, 35, 41, 82, 91, 101, 121, 126, 151
Still, 91, 107, 114, 116, 117, 120, 126, 130, 137, 151, 154

Sting, 44
Stirred, 117
Stirs, 155
Stocking, 77
Stockings, 121
Stones, 80, 135
Stood, 93, 97, 105, 106, 110, 116
Stooped, 83
Stop, 77
Stores, 136
Stories, 123, 129, 131
Story, 123, 149
Stove, 144
Straight, 67
Strands, 85
Strange, 99, 145
Strapped, 107
Straw, 105
Stream, 102, 141, 147
Streams, 147
Street, 126
Streets, 59
Strength, 74
Stretch, 154
Stripe, 77
Strolling, 111
Strong, 60, 117, 120
Strong-minded, 150
Students, 18
Studied, 119
Study, 103
Stuff, 50
Stuffed, 77
Stumbled, 142
Subject, 79
Succeed, 24
Success, 111
Such, 89, 102, 107, 114, 123, 125, 152, 154
Suddenly, 116, 145, 154
Suffering, 119
Sufficient, 150
Sufficiently, 150
Sugar, 118
Suit, 86
Suitable, 104
Suitcase, 77
Summer, 62, 96, 126, 132, 136, 154
Summer's, 111, 136
Sun, 62, 125, 138, 139, 145, 146, 154
Sunday, 47
Sung, 141
Sunk, 76
Sunset, 146
Sunshine, 119, 149
Supper, 57
Sure, 23, 94, 98, 111, 127, 156
Surefooted, 122
Surely, 130
Surface, 80, 119, 142, 147
Surprise, 67
Suspect, 152, 156

Swaying, 149
Sweet, 72, 95, 129, 149, 150, 155, 157
Sweetly, 149
Swift, 78, 80
Swiftly, 120
Swine's, 51
Swing, 113
Swinging, 139
Swinton's, 80, 89, 95, 103

T

Table, 41, 57, 130
Tag, 134
Tail, 112, 134, 138, 152
Take, 86, 101, 140, 156
Taken, 131, 151
Takes, 134
Taking, 136
Tale, 123
Tales, 123
Talk, 68
Talking, 69, 82
Tame, 122
Tangled, 52
Tap, 123
Taste, 150
Taxi, 77
Taylor, 54
Teach, 137
Teaches, 32
Teapot, 123
Tears, 115
Teeth, 99
Telephone, 94
Tell, 102, 117, 123, 124, 138, 139, 140, 149
Temper, 107
Temptation, 150
Tempting, 111
Ten, 87
Tender, 102, 150
Tennyson, 141
Terms, 151
Terrible, 150
Than, 19, 74, 80, 85, 98, 103, 113, 124, 129, 140, 151, 154, 156
Thank, 60
Thankful, 108
Thanksgiving, 108
That, 37, 40, 43, 49, 50, 53, 59, 63, 64, 71, 81, 86, 87, 88, 93, 94, 95, 99, 100, 104, 106, 108, 109, 112, 114, 116, 118, 119, 120, 121, 123, 124, 127, 128, 129, 131, 135, 136, 137, 138, 140, 142, 143, 147, 148, 150, 151, 152, 153, 154, 156
That's, 69, 134
Thatch, 141
Thaws, 155
The, 22, 23, 25, 27, 29, 32, 33, 35, 36, 37, 40, 43, 46, 48, 50, 53, 54, 55, 57, 58, 59, 60, 62, 63, 64, 66,

67, 68, 69, 70, 71, 72, 73, 74, 76, 77, 78, 79, 80, 81, 82, 83, 84, 85, 86, 87, 88, 89, 90, 91, 92, 93, 94, 95, 96, 97, 99, 100, 101, 102, 103, 104, 105, 106, 107, 108, 109, 110, 111, 112, 113, 114, 115, 116, 117, 118, 119, 120, 121, 122, 123, 124, 125, 126, 127, 129, 130, 131, 132, 133, 134, 135, 136, 137, 138, 139, 140, 141, 142, 143, 144, 145, 146, 147, 148, 149, 150, 151, 152, 153, 154, 155, 156, 157
Thee, 44, 60, 72, 102
Their, 28, 73, 86, 89, 95, 96, 103, 104, 110, 112, 113, 115, 116, 122, 127, 146, 152, 155
Them, 39, 65, 68, 86, 96, 119, 123, 124, 131, 138, 146, 150, 151, 153, 157
Themselves, 105, 113, 123
Then, 50, 67, 83, 88, 89, 98, 109, 116, 118, 132, 136, 137, 139, 142, 146, 151, 154, 155
There, 27, 40, 71, 74, 80, 81, 91, 93, 97, 99, 101, 105, 109, 119, 123, 124, 129, 131, 133, 135, 139, 149, 154, 156
There's, 56
Therefore, 137, 148, 154
These, 63, 74, 75, 79, 89, 119, 121, 125, 133, 138, 140, 145, 152
They, 28, 39, 57, 63, 73, 86, 93, 96, 101, 103, 104, 105, 110, 111, 112, 113, 115, 116, 117, 118, 122, 123, 130, 134, 136, 137, 145, 146, 150, 152, 153
They're, 98
Thick, 110
Thin, 110
Thing, 107, 111, 132, 135, 137, 145
Things, 23, 36, 54, 65, 73, 75, 93, 99, 150
Think, 35, 37, 124, 138, 140, 147
Thinking, 55, 100
Third, 101
Thirst, 111, 154
Thirsty, 98, 154
Thirty, 66
Thirty-one, 66
This, 60, 70, 74, 87, 97, 99, 101, 103, 110, 119, 128, 132, 137, 138, 139, 140, 142, 145, 147, 150, 15?, 154
Thistle, 143
Thomas, 30
Thorn, 84
Thornton, 124, 129, 131, 142, 150, 152, 156
Those, 62, 103, 119, 124, 152
Thou, 42, 44, 50, 74, 102, 114, 130
Though, 56, 83, 121, 122, 130, 137, 144

Thought, 23, 35, 94, 98, 117, 127, 138, 142
Thoughts, 110
Thousand, 31
Thread, 85, 86, 132, 133
Thread-like, 147
Threatened, 59
Three, 111, 133, 138, 140
Thrice, 141
Through, 110, 111, 117, 130, 138, 157
Throughout, 127
Throw, 134
Thursday, 47
Thy, 39, 74, 102, 130
Thyself, 42, 74
Tiger, 122
Tight, 73, 143
Tightly, 107
Till, 66, 72, 92, 111, 115, 118, 134
Time, 50, 69, 92, 101, 118, 121, 124, 127, 129, 134, 135, 145, 156
Times, 139, 154
Timid, 156
Timidity, 152
Tin, 78
Tiniest, 156
Tint, 95
Tiny, 103, 119, 145, 147, 149
Tired, 137, 154
To, 28, 32, 34, 35, 41, 52, 55, 57, 59, 64, 67, 71, 75, 76, 77, 79, 81, 82, 83, 85, 86, 87, 89, 90, 91, 92, 93, 94, 95, 99, 100, 101, 103, 105, 107, 108, 109, 110, 111, 112, 113, 114, 115, 117, 118, 119, 120, 121, 122, 123, 124, 125, 126, 127, 128, 129, 130, 131, 132, 134, 135, 136, 137, 138, 139, 140, 142, 143, 144, 146, 147, 150, 151, 152, 153, 154, 155, 156, 157
Today, 143
Toe, 77
Together, 89, 110, 129, 132, 135, 150
Toil, 63, 136
Toiling, 136
Told, 112
Tomorrow, 42, 48, 92
Tongue, 46
Tonight, 69
Too, 64, 71, 87, 88, 95, 117, 156
Took, 97, 111, 118
Tools, 99, 117
Top, 93, 97, 106, 133, 139
Touch, 143
Toward, 125, 150
Towel, 81
Traffic, 77, 87
Trained, 111
Traitor, 91
Transition, 64
Trap, 112
Travel, 55

Treasure, 82, 91, 101, 121, 151, 157
Treat, 155
Tree, 29, 73, 89, 99, 116, 117, 126, 148
Trees, 106, 113, 150, 154, 157
Tremble, 116
Trick, 124
Trickles, 80
Tricks, 124
Tried, 111
Trifle, 151
Trip, 31, 142
Troop, 116
Trot, 137, 143
Trouble, 128, 150
Troubled, 127
True, 41
Trust, 32
Truth, 46, 108
Try, 24, 124, 156
Tuesday, 47
Tulips, 155
Tunnel, 142
Turn, 101, 151
Turned, 123, 144, 146, 150
Turning, 111
Turnip, 89
Turns, 147
Twelve, 140
Twice, 44, 115, 141
Twig, 117
Twilight, 104
Twines, 113
Twinkle, 150
Twinkling, 138, 149
Twist, 27
Two, 79, 83, 109, 111, 113, 118, 119, 133, 138, 152

U

Ugly, 73
Umbrella, 70
Umbrellas, 29
Unable, 127
Unbroke, 120
Under, 117, 131, 135, 152
Understand, 83
Understanding, 49
Understands, 79
Understood, 142
Underwater, 131
Uneasy, 116
Unfastened, 83
Unfit, 127
Ungodly, 148
Unhappy, 156
Unknown, 47, 60, 66, 96
Unlike, 122, 152
Unpacking, 107
Unpromising, 117
Until, 101, 122, 147
Unto, 45, 63, 108
Unweariedly, 82

Up, 25, 28, 59, 79, 80, 81, 82, 86, 90, 97, 100, 105, 107, 111, 112, 113, 115, 118, 126, 128, 129, 135, 136, 142, 146, 147, 151, 153, 156
Upon, 105, 112, 118, 119, 123, 141, 145, 154
Upper, 152
Upset, 116
Upstairs, 121
Us, 54, 69, 78, 94, 95, 101, 108, 121, 124, 125, 128, 129, 140, 145, 154, 157
Use, 64, 69, 117, 140
Used, 36, 81, 99, 109, 140
Useful, 117, 134
Uses, 83
Usual, 152

V

Vain, 153
Vales, 102, 157
Valley, 130
Vapor, 144, 145, 146, 147
Varies, 109
Variety, 43
Vast, 110, 154
Venice, 44
Ventures, 156
Very, 35, 43, 97, 109, 117, 131, 133, 134, 137, 143, 146, 150, 156
Vices, 61
Vine, 111, 118
Vines, 157
Violets, 149
Visitor, 76
Visits, 157
Voice, 78, 102, 129
Vow, 143
Vowels, 78
Voyage, 55

W

Wadsworth, 120
Wag, 134
Wagon, 138
Wait, 156
Waited, 156
Waiting, 152, 156
Waketh, 153
Waldo, 32, 33, 36, 37
Walk, 105, 122, 130, 137, 140
Walked, 111
Walketh, 148
Walking, 53
Walter, 52
Wander, 131
Want, 58, 128, 130, 152
Wanted, 94, 99, 105, 151
Wanting, 95
Wants, 97
War, 61, 135
Warm, 155
Warming, 141
Warning, 115

Was, 58, 59, 62, 63, 64, 71, 73, 81, 82, 83, 86, 87, 90, 91, 92, 93, 99, 100, 104, 106, 107, 110, 111, 112, 115, 116, 117, 118, 121, 124, 127, 128, 131, 136, 138, 142, 150, 151, 152
Wash, 47
Wasn, 142
Waste, 69
Wasted, 151
Watch, 53, 103
Watched, 112, 124
Watcher, 112
Watching, 124
Watchman, 153
Water, 80, 98, 100, 106, 109, 123, 131, 144, 145, 146, 147, 148, 149, 154
Waters, 130
Waving, 154
Way, 75, 82, 89, 100, 119, 125, 126, 136, 137, 142, 147, 148
Ways, 122
We, 23, 52, 56, 60, 69, 78, 87, 97, 101, 102, 106, 108, 109, 123, 124, 125, 128, 136, 138, 139, 140, 144, 145, 146, 147, 154, 156
We're, 151
Wealth, 91
Wealthy, 34
Wear, 137
Weariness, 137
Weather, 59, 70
Weave, 52
Weavers, 127
Web, 52, 85
Wednesday, 47
Weep, 135
Well, 36, 97, 98, 106, 143, 151, 152, 154
Went, 81, 83, 96, 105, 117, 118, 136
Were, 73, 86, 91, 96, 104, 110, 117, 118, 127, 151, 154
West, 125, 129, 131, 138, 139, 157
What, 20, 37, 42, 44, 52, 55, 65, 67, 87, 92, 101, 105, 114, 116, 124, 125, 133, 137, 139, 144, 150, 152, 157
What's, 41
Whatever, 121
Whatsoever, 148
Wheat, 150
When, 40, 41, 52, 53, 55, 62, 90, 92, 99, 101, 103, 107, 112, 115, 116, 117, 118, 119, 121, 125, 126, 127, 129, 131, 136, 137, 139, 140, 141, 144, 146, 150, 151, 152, 154, 156
Whenever, 105
Where, 72, 109, 120, 124, 125, 139, 140, 144, 145, 146, 147, 150
Whether, 85

Which, 27, 39, 48, 51, 66, 82, 83, 86, 91, 93, 97, 98, 104, 106, 107, 109, 110, 111, 121, 122, 129, 132, 133, 135, 139, 142, 145, 147, 148, 154

While, 59, 117, 118, 136, 137, 152

Whirling, 96, 155

Whirring, 141

Whistle, 129

White, 83, 95, 113, 141, 149, 152, 157

Whitefoot, 152, 156

Who, 33, 40, 54, 79, 102, 103, 113, 119, 120, 152

Whole, 41, 70, 83, 86, 116, 152

Why, 136

Wide, 140, 147, 149, 154

Wife, 151

Wild, 154

Wilder, 128

Will, 18, 53, 85, 87, 89, 92, 95, 124, 128, 130, 132, 137, 138, 143, 144, 147

William, 43, 90, 102

Willows, 83, 107

Wind, 55, 62, 80, 83, 96, 107, 129, 131, 148, 151, 157

Wind's, 96

Windowpanes, 157

Windows, 55

Winds, 147, 157

Wing, 84, 119

Winsome, 129

Winter, 62, 96, 126, 136

Wisdom, 156

Wise, 34, 127

Wish, 90, 137, 140, 143

Wishes, 137

With, 21, 31, 33, 35, 60, 61, 67, 71, 74, 76, 77, 81, 84, 86, 89, 91, 94, 96, 99, 100, 103, 104, 106, 108, 111, 114, 116, 117, 118, 121, 122, 124, 127, 130, 132, 133, 134, 136, 138, 139, 140, 143, 146, 147, 151, 152, 153, 154, 155

Wither, 148

Within, 78, 83

Without, 51, 86, 107, 115, 137, 156, 157

Wits, 124, 141

Wolfgang, 143

Woman, 51, 137

Womb, 153

Women, 118

Won't, 123, 128

Wonder, 91

Wonderful, 124, 127

Wood, 65, 117, 152, 156

Woodcutting, 99

Woods, 53

Woolly, 102

Word, 79, 101, 128, 151

Words, 49, 79

Wordsworth, 90

Work, 33, 47, 85, 99, 104, 107, 115, 127, 142

Workers, 85

Works, 33, 134

World, 23, 35, 48, 80, 84, 85, 93, 122, 150, 156

Worst, 36, 137

Worth, 128

Worthy, 22

Would, 91, 101, 110, 115, 116, 117, 127, 128, 140, 146, 151, 156

Wouldn't, 93

Wouldst, 44

Woven, 132, 133

Wrinkled, 98

Write, 143

Wrong, 87, 151

Wrote, 121

X, Y, Z

Yard, 140

Yardstick, 140

Ye, 45, 108

Yea, 130

Year, 61, 66, 129, 156, 157

Year's, 84

Yellow, 95, 126, 132

Yes, 97, 115, 123, 150

Yesterday, 142

Yet, 48, 63, 83, 97, 127

Yield, 150

Yielding, 150

You, 20, 24, 30, 45, 53, 61, 63, 65, 67, 68, 69, 78, 87, 88, 92, 123, 126, 128, 132, 133, 136, 137, 138, 139, 140, 143, 145, 146, 150, 152, 153, 156

You'll, 78

Young, 69, 79, 103, 109, 112, 132, 150

Younger, 110

Your, 21, 30, 61, 87, 88, 96, 125, 132, 140, 143, 150

Youth, 153